MW00437460

THE
A–TO–Z GUIDE
TO
EVENT
FUNDRAISING

AMY S. CROWELL, CFRE

Edited by: Ben Beach

© 2017 Amy S. Crowell, CFRE

All Rights Reserved.

Reproduction or translation of any part of this work beyond that permitted by Section 107 or 108 of the 1976 United States Copyright Act without permission of the copyright owner is unlawful. Requests for permission or further information should be addressed to Next Stage Advisors.

Next State Advisors

NextStageAdv.com
770-609-7188

Dog Ear Publishing
4011 Vincennes Rd
Indianapolis, IN 46268
www.dogearpublishing.net

ISBN: 978-1-4575-5070-6

This book is printed on acid-free paper.

Printed in the United States of America

This book is dedicated to all the non-profit pros and volunteers who work hard to make their communities a better place.

Special thanks to my husband, Ken, and my children, Sam, Nicholas, and Julianna. Without them, I would never have been inspired to work in non-profit or believe a book was in my future.

TABLE OF CONTENTS

INTRODUCTION

C ongratulations on your decision to embark on the fulfilling journey toward helping your nonprofit organization raise funds for its important mission. For you, nothing is more essential than making a positive impact in the community. While there are numerous ways to attract funding to a nonprofit, this book focuses on how a well-planned and well-marketed event can help your organization raise revenue.

The A-to-Z Guide to Event Fundraising will lead you from start to finish, beginning with helping you choose which type of event will work best for your organization. It will guide you through the planning, the event itself, and the follow-up. It will teach you not only how to maximize revenue, but also how to recognize the secondary benefits your event can yield, such as increasing public awareness of your organization and attracting new supporters.

The book is divided into five sections. The first two chapters will help you decide why you should host an event fundraiser and define the goals you wish to accomplish for your organization. We will discuss the most common (and some less common) types of events and what you should consider when deciding which type to host. *The A-to-Z Guide to Event Fundraising* will also give you many unique ideas for making your event stand out from the crowd and attract more sponsors and attendees.

The next five chapters focus on revenue. Events raise money through three main streams: sponsorships, ticket or participant revenue and auctions. Chapters 3 through 7 provide an in-depth look at each of these revenue streams (plus a few others), while teaching you everything you need to know about them. You'll learn how to price different sponsor levels and which benefits to offer those sponsors, how to price tickets and participant fees, what types of auction items sell best and even how to expand your in-kind donations.

Chapters 8 through 10 introduce you to the people who can help make your event a success. We'll look at the way boards of directors, volunteers and media and public relations specialists play essential roles in every event's success.

Chapters 11 and 12 take a deeper look into why hosting an event differs from other types of fundraising, such as individual giving or grant writing. You'll see how events have the amazing ability to create a new set of organizational supporters – and how your event can encourage existing supporters to move to a deeper level of involvement. These chapters unlock the secrets of how to create loyalty to your cause by showing attendees how your organization is helping the community. You'll learn everything you need to know to ensure continued communication and relationship-building with your attendees after the event ends.

Finally, chapters 13 through 15 touch upon essential components of any event. First, the importance of organizing logistics to ensure that your event is as smooth and stress-free as possible. You'll even learn proven techniques that will help you separate the "nice-to-haves" from the necessities, thereby saving money and netting more funds for your organization. Chapter 14 will guide you through the week surrounding your event, providing guidance and a checklist to ensure you don't miss anything important. At the end, we'll discuss the need for a thorough post-event analysis so that the next time your event is even better. We'll show you how to review the different areas of your event and even consider whether you would be wise to hire paid help, discontinue the event or reinvent it.

In addition to the book, we have a downloadable appendix (available at docs.*AtoZEventFundraising.com*) that contains many useful tools, checklists, sample documents and worksheets to help you stay organized as you work on your event. It will take you step by step, from the day-one decision-making moment to the completion of the event (and beyond!).

Congratulations again for your commitment to your organization and its goals and for the hard work you do to help the people, pets, environment or the community that your nonprofit serves.

Section One

The Basics of Event Fundraising

*To get your FREE copy of the A-to-Z Guide to Event Fundraising appendix
full of useful tools, checklists, sample document and worksheets, visit*
docs.AtoZEventFundraising.com.

CHAPTER

1

WHY FUNDRAISE VIA EVENTS?

In This Chapter

- ✔ What is an event fundraiser?

- ✔ What your organization can achieve from an event

- ✔ Essentials for event fundraising

- ✔ When you should choose event fundraising

- ✔ Challenges of event fundraising

- ✔ How money is raised at events

Fundraising is vital for any nonprofit, and there are many ways for organizations to raise funds. The options include grants, individual giving, planned giving and more. But events also have a place in the mix and often deliver benefits that other fundraising methods cannot. We will explore some of those benefits and examine how events, while not always the easiest way to raise money, can be just what your organization needs.

What is an Event Fundraiser?

An **event fundraiser** is an event whose main purpose is to generate additional funds for your organization. It could be a 5K walk/run, a seated dinner, a food-tasting, a golf tournament or any other type of event. Beyond bringing in revenue, events usually provide other benefits, including greater awareness of your nonprofit, new supporters and deeper relationships with existing supporters.

> *event fundraiser:* an event whose main purpose is to generate revenue

There are many different types of event fundraisers. A few of the most common are listed below, along with examples. (See Chapter 2 for detailed information about these events.)

Athletic Events

- Run/walk/bike event - 5K, 10K, half-marathon, marathon, triathlon

- Sports tournaments – golf, basketball, baseball

- A-thons – dance, bike, bowling

Food and Beverage Events

- Seated dinner gala

- Food-and-wine tasting

- Food-and-wine festival

- Cooking demonstration

Other

- One-day/night events – talent show, battle of the bands, casino night, fashion show, trivia night

- Family-friendly events – carnival, festival, touch-a-truck, ice cream social, pancake breakfast

- Miscellaneous – baseball games or other ticketed events, restaurant fundraiser nights

What Your Organization Can Achieve from an Event

Events have the unique ability to not only raise funds, but to also achieve numerous other benefits. Some of the most common benefits are:

Net revenue

Revenue includes any funds from ticket sales or registrations, sponsorships, auctions, donations and other funds the event brings in. Net revenue is revenue remaining after you subtract the direct (and sometimes indirect) expenses of putting on the event. Direct event expenses include venue fees, food and beverages, T-shirts, signs and anything else that you must pay for. An example of an indirect expense would be if your staff person paid $40,000 per year spends 25 percent of her time planning the event, $10,000 would be an indirect cost. Industry best practice states that direct expenses should be no more than 30 percent of what is raised, but many organizations keep it in the 15-20 percent range.

Unrestricted dollars

Unlike many grants and large donations, event fundraising dollars are often **unrestricted revenue**. Unrestricted money can be spent on anything that the organization chooses, including both programmatic and non-programmatic expenses. Non-programmatic expenses such as rent, utilities and salaries for people not directly running your programs can often be harder to fundraise for than programmatic expenses. Salaries for individuals leading your programs, cost for materials used during your programs, etc. are all considered programmatic expenses and can often be paid for with **restricted revenue** raised from grants or major donations.

unrestricted revenue: money given to an organization that can be used as the organization chooses

restricted revenue: funds given to an organization that can only be used for a specific, predetermined purpose

Organizational awareness

Larger-scale events, especially ones that are well promoted through public relations and/or advertising (See Chapter 10), can help you increase the number of people aware of your organization and the problems it is working to solve. New attendees, of course, will learn more at your event, but even those who do not attend may become interested when they see information about your event and may take steps to learn more. Few other fundraising methods have the potential to create the level of awareness that events do.

New volunteers

Event attendees may come to your event knowing little or nothing about your organization. By demonstrating your organization's impact in the community at the event (See Chapter 11) and performing the right follow-up (See Chapter 15), you can bring in new volunteers to help your mission.

Connections or introductions to people who can help your organization

Events are a great way to introduce potential supporters to your organization. Do you have a short list of people you'd like to become supporters, such as philanthropists known to give to organizations similar to yours? Well known and respected community members? Ask current supporters to invite anyone on your list they know (or others you may not know) so you can introduce them to your organization and its mission. A spark of interest that occurs at an event can be fanned at a later date when you have more time to tell them about your organization and learn how they may be interested in helping.

An opportunity to thank, further engage or re-engage existing donors and volunteers

Events are fun for attendees! Inviting them to your event (especially one where you show all the wonderful work your organization is doing in a compelling way) is a great opportunity to show appreciation for your donors and volunteers and remind them why they are helping. They may be so inspired that they want to do even more!

Done well, your event can reap all these benefits and more, while helping your organization in ways well beyond fundraising.

Essentials for an Event

No matter what type of event you host, there are a few essentials, including:

Location

Depending on your event, this could be a hotel or event venue, a golf course, auditorium, outdoor space or a variety of other options.

Food and beverage

This can vary widely depending on the type of event, from water and bananas at a 5K to a 3-course seated dinner at a black-tie gala.

Seed money

Your organization will need to have some funds available for deposits or expenses that must be paid for early in the planning process. Venues, food and beverage and printing often need to be paid prior to collecting any sponsor or attendee revenue and many are non-refundable, even if the event is cancelled or raises less revenue than anticipated.

Time

Events are time-consuming and often need numerous people to make them a success. You will spend many hours handling logistics, soliciting sponsors, attracting participants, gathering live and/or silent auction items and more.

Information about your organization's impact

It is important to inform your guests about your organization and how it is helping your community. It is typically both quantitative ("1,000 people successfully graduated from our program and improved their reading levels by 30 percent.") and non-quantitative ("Our students not only learn to read; they also increase their confidence levels and do better in school overall."). It can be demonstrated in numerous forms, including signs, PowerPoint presentations, videos and in-person speakers. (See Chapter 11.)

When You Should Choose Event Fundraising

There are numerous ways for nonprofits to raise money, and it's a fair argument that event fundraising is one of the most time-intensive, least-bang-for-your–buck options. While it is certainly more difficult to organize a 200-person seated dinner with a live and silent auction to raise $150,000, it isn't always possible to get one or more people to write checks to your organization for the same $150,000. So, when should you and your staff put your energy toward an event versus doubling up on your grant writing or major donor work? Below are components that give an event a higher probability of success. You don't need all of them, but having more helps.

Ample human capital

Having enough staff, volunteers, board members or others willing to pitch in can go a long way toward event success.

A sizable database

Success is more likely if you have enough supporters in your database to reach your goal for participation. What is enough? According to MailChimp, an email marketing company, nonprofits average an **open rate** of 25.29 percent and a **click-through rate** of 2.85 percent. To see if your database is close to what you need, plug your goals into this example:

open rate: the number of people on an email list that view an email campaign

click-through rate: the percentage of people who click on one of your links in an email

An organization is hosting a 5K race with the goal of 100 runners and an email list of 3,500 names. Using the stats above:

- 885 people would open the email (Open rate = 3,500 X 25.29%)

- About 100 would click through to get more information (Click through rate = 3,500 X 2.85%)

Since 100 percent wouldn't actually register, the nonprofit would need a list larger than 3,500 to obtain 100 registrations, unless the organization had other means to get runners.

A responsive database

Even if your database isn't large, if your supporters have a good record of responding to your communications, you may be able to hit your target. When you send a group email, are your open rates high? Do you get a click-through rate even higher than the 2.85 percent industry average mentioned above? Does your list naturally lend itself to drawing attendees to the type of event you are hosting, for example a health organization that is hosting a 5K or health fair. If your audience is not very engaged, it may be more challenging to hit your ticket or attendee goals, especially if the ticket price is high.

Seed money

Having the budget or a sponsor or benefactor who commits early to most, if not all, of your initial expenses helps immensely. Also, increasing the number of in-kind donations or partial donations for event expenses (e.g., food, beverage, A/V, décor) increases the likelihood of high net revenue.

While all four of these items are not required in order to have a profitable event, having more of them will not only increase your chances of success, but will reduce the time your staff spends on the event and the overall stress. If you feel you are lacking in one or more of these areas, don't give up! Your board of directors and volunteers should be able to help you overcome many of these challenges. And if they can't, that doesn't mean you shouldn't host an event. It may just mean that you should choose a smaller event, such as a seated dinner for 100 in a restaurant, versus a food-and-wine event for 1,000 with multiple chefs.

Challenges of Event Fundraising

No fundraising is ever easy. When trying to decide if an event fundraiser is best for your organization, consider some of these more common event challenges.

They take time.

There are a lot of details to manage (especially for first-time events), which can drain staff and/or volunteer time.

Potentially unreliable volunteers

Even if you set up a strong and deep committee, it consists of volunteers who are just that – volunteers. Other life situations will invariably arise, making them less than 100 percent reliable. Plan to recruit 15 to 20 percent more volunteers than you think you will need. (See Chapter 9.)

Events can be expensive.

There are many fixed costs, especially compared to other types of fundraising such as grant writing or individual giving campaigns. Many of these financial commitments have to be made even if your attendance is disappointing. For example, if you organize a seated dinner, you likely will have to sign a contract with the venue for not only a flat fee to rent the room, but typically a food and beverage minimum as well.

Fundraising vs. logistics

When planning an event, it is extremely easy to get mired in the "must do" logistics of your event and not spend enough time on the fundraising component. Events have a long series of "to-do's" with hard deadlines. Keeping fundraising first and foremost for you and the committee, although difficult, is a necessity to maximize your event's financial success.

How Money Is Raised at Events

Event fundraisers have a variety of revenue streams. The most common are:

Sponsorships

These are funds raised in support of your event from individuals (sometimes called "patrons") or companies. In selling sponsorships, you will need to create a menu-style list (often called a "deck"), which specifies the different sponsor levels and the benefits that sponsors receive for each level of financial commitment. The more the sponsor gives, the more benefits that sponsor receives. Companies or people may sponsor your event for a variety of reasons. Some may be committed to your cause, while others may think the event is a good marketing opportunity or a great way to entertain clients. This is often one of the largest revenue sources and, ideally, it will cover the hard costs of the event, allowing the other revenue streams to go straight to your nonprofit's bottom line. (See Chapter 3.)

Participant revenue

This can come in various forms, but basically it is the money paid by people to attend your event. It's an entry fee for a 5K, a ticket price for a seated dinner or a registration fee for a golf tournament. (See Chapter 4.)

Auctions

Many events use an auction to raise additional money. Auctions come in all shapes and sizes from live auctions (where items are sold by an auctioneer and attendees bid on the spot) to small or expansive silent auctions (where items are bid on by guests throughout the event via paper bid sheets or through their smartphones). Auctions can be a lot of work but can raise substantial funds. (See Chapter 5.)

Donations

Asking your attendees to make a donation is another common way to increase your revenue. You can ask for the donation at the event via a "paddle raise" or "fund the need," where cash donations are requested live during the event program, typically by the auctioneer. Other common ways are via peer-to-peer fundraising (participants are asked to set a goal to raise $XX from families and friends when they sign up for the event), by requesting an additional donation while at the event or when purchasing a ticket. (See Chapter 6 for information about donations and other event revenue sources.)

By saving expenses

Another way to make money is not to spend it. There are numerous ways to be careful about what you buy and how and what to solicit donations for to help you cut your costs. Anything you can avoid paying for goes straight to your organization to help fulfill its mission. (See Chapter 7.)

Now that you know a bit more about the types of event fundraisers, what you need, what can be achieved and the variety of ways you will raise money, it's time to look more closely at each event type, how to choose the most promising one and what you can do to make yours stand out from the crowd.

Chapter To-Do List

✔ **Review event essentials list and when you should choose event fundraising information.**

✔ **Determine if hosting an event is the best way to fundraise for your organization.**

2

TYPES OF EVENT FUNDRAISERS: CHOOSING AN EVENT TYPE AND MAKING IT SHINE

In This Chapter

- ✔ **Information about types of events, each of their revenue streams, expenses, pros and cons**

- ✔ **How to choose which type of event**

- ✔ **How to make your event stand out**

There is a wide variety of events. Below is a summary of the most popular options and the pros/cons and potential revenue sources for each.

Athletic Events

Whether your organization hosts a run/walk, a golf tournament or a different event, athletic events are a popular option. They are fairly easy to put on and are attractive to a large number of people, primarily because the entry fee tends to be modest.

Type of Event	Potential Revenue Streams	Potential Expenses	Pros	Cons
Athletic Events				
Run/walk/bike - 5K, 10K, half-marathon, marathon, triathlon, 1-miler, children's race or other distance	Sponsorship, entry fees, peer-to-peer fundraising, team fundraising, donations, potentially an auction or raffle	Race director, items needed to put on a race, such as timing chips, cones, staff, bib numbers, etc. (if your race director doesn't provide them), T-shirts, signs, food, ice, graphic design, security, winners' medals, plaques or other prizes, marketing (flyers, website, Facebook ads), postage, insurance, potentially tents, tables	• A large number of people can potentially run/walk. • Entry fees are relatively small compared to other events. • Peer-to-peer or team fundraising can bring in more funds and supporters. • Time needed from staff or volunteers is less than for other events, especially if you hire a race director.	• Races are often a commodity with walkers or runners choosing races due to convenience or location rather than commitment to your cause; without a special draw (for example, a great goody bag or a flat course), it can be difficult to attract runners and walkers. • Weather can significantly impact number of entries.
Sports tournaments -golf, basketball, baseball, etc.	Sponsorship, individual and team registration, peer-to-peer fundraising, contests, donations, auction or raffle, merchandise sales, dinner tickets, if hosted	Venue or facility course fees, labor, decorations, food and beverage, signs, prizes, insurance, marketing (flyers, website), gifts, postage, merchandise	• Tournaments are often considered business expenses, so it may be easier to get entrants than for another type of event, especially golf if held during the week. • Relatively easy to organize	• If tournaments are during working hours and participants aren't going as part of their job, it may be difficult to get attendees. • Venue fee can be more expensive than other types of events
A-thons - dance, bike, rock (as in rocking chairs), bowling, dodgeball, etc.: last person or couple doing the activity wins	Sponsorship, entry fees, peer-to-peer fundraising, team fundraising, donations, auction or raffle	Venue, entertainment, signs, graphic design, security, winners' medals, plaques or other prizes, marketing (flyers, website, Facebook ads), postage, insurance	• Event is relatively easy to organize. • A-thons are less common, making it potentially easier to get entrants.	• If someone doesn't enjoy the activity, she/he likely won't participate. • If peer-to-peer fundraising isn't embraced, net proceeds may be low.

Food and Beverage Events

Food and beverage fundraisers often raise a large amount of money, but they usually take more time to organize, depending on numerous variables, as outlined below.

Type of Event	Potential Revenue Streams	Potential Expenses	Pros	Cons
Food and Beverage Events				
Seated dinner/gala	Sponsorships or patrons, table sales, individual ticket sales, donations, live or silent auction, raffle	Venue rental, food and beverage, labor, internet access, signs, insurance, supplies, marketing (flyers, website). Potentially rentals (tables, chairs, linens, flatware, glassware, tent), event planner, A/V rental and labor, dance floor, entertainment, alcohol license, auction software, security, parking, valet, transportation for special guests, postage, gifts	• Can be a high revenue producer • Stage presentations provide opportunity to share mission and impact information. • Great way to thank/engage/steward best volunteers and donors • Engaging way to bring in new supporters or move current ones to the next level of support	• Time-consuming, lots of details to manage • Labor-intensive, staff, volunteers or both • Large up-front expenses, many of them fixed
Food-and-wine tasting or festival	Sponsorship, ticket sales, donations, live or silent auction, raffle	Venue rental, food and beverage, labor, internet access, signs, insurance, supplies, marketing (flyers, website). Potentially rentals (tables, chairs, linens, flatware, glassware, tent, dance floor), event planner, A/V rental and labor, auction software, security, entertainment, alcohol license, parking, valet, transportation for special guests, postage, gifts	• Can be a high revenue producer • Stage presentations provide opportunity to share mission and impact information. • Great way to thank/engage/steward great volunteers and donors • Engaging way to bring in new supporters or move current ones to the next level of support	• Time-consuming, lots of details to manage • Labor-intensive for staff, volunteers or both • If an outdoor event, weather can significantly impact attendance.

Type of Event	Potential Revenue Streams	Potential Expenses	Pros	Cons
Food and Beverage Events				
Cooking demonstrations	Sponsorships or patrons, table sales, individual ticket sales, donations, live or silent auction, raffle	Venue rental, labor, A/V rental and labor, stage, signs, insurance, supplies, marketing (flyers, website). Potentially food and beverage, rentals (chairs, glassware, flatware, tent, etc.), event planner, auction software, security, alcohol license, parking, valet, transportation for special guests, postage, gifts	• Usually less work than other food and beverage events • Can be a high revenue producer • Stage presentations provide opportunity to share mission and impact information. • Great way to thank/engage/steward best volunteers and donors • Engaging way to bring in new supporters or move current ones to the next level of support • Ticket price is likely lower than for other food and beverage events so may attract more people.	• Needs to have the right draw to be a success • Revenue may be less than other food and beverage events (lower ticket price, etc.)

Other Events

Beyond the normal athletic or food and beverage events, there are countless other types of events. Here are a few ideas to get you started. But let your imagination wander: The sky is the limit!

Type of Event	Potential Revenue Streams	Potential Expenses	Pros	Cons
Other Events				
One-day/night event - talent show, battle of the bands, casino night, trivia contest, health fair	Sponsorship, ticket sales, donations, live or silent auction, raffle	Venue rental, labor, A/V rental and labor, entertainment (e.g., casino staff, band or DJ), signs, insurance, supplies, marketing (flyers, website), food and beverage, rentals (tent, stage, tables, chairs, linens, tableware, décor, flooring, etc.), event planner, auction software, security, alcohol license, parking, valet, transportation for special guests, postage, gifts.	• Different from typical gala-type events so may attract more people • Ticket price is likely on lower end so may attract more and new people. • Stage presentations provide opportunity to share mission and impact information. • Great way to thank/engage/ steward best volunteers and donors • Engaging way to bring in new supporters or move current ones to the next level of support	• Talent shows and battles of the bands are complicated due to numerous acts. • May not be as appealing to corporate sponsors because not as "client-friendly" • Can be more expensive to put on than other events (for example casino night staff, additional labor for set changes, etc.) • May be more difficult to incorporate auctions or donation opportunities
Family-friendly event - carnival, trivia night, etc.	Sponsorship, ticket sales, donations, live or silent auction, raffle	Venue rental, labor, A/V rental and labor, entertainment (e.g., carnival staff), signs, insurance, supplies, marketing (flyers, website), food and beverage, rentals (tent, stage, tables, chairs, linens, tableware, décor, flooring, etc.), event planner, auction software, security, parking, postage, gifts.	• Family-friendly events open up an entirely new set of potential attendees, which may be especially good if your organization helps children. • Great way to bring in people new to the organization • Ticket price is likely on lower end so may attract more people.	• Ticket price likely needs to be low to attract families, so revenue potential from that source is also lower. • Events with multiple components (for example, stage presentation, booths, etc.) can be time-consuming to organize. • May be difficult to have a live or silent auction depending on type of event • If outdoors, weather can effect attendance

Type of Event	Potential Revenue Streams	Potential Expenses	Pros	Cons
Other Events				
Miscellaneous - baseball game (for example, discounted tickets are provided to a nonprofit and any amount the tickets are sold for above that amount benefits the organization), restaurant fundraiser, etc.	Ticket sales, percentage of sales at the restaurant that evening, donations	Ticket price, potentially cost per person paid to the restaurant, marketing (flyers, website, etc.)	Fairly easy to organize	• Revenue potential smaller than many of the other options • If you have to sell a minimum number of tickets, you may lose money if you don't sell them all. • Not a lot of opportunity to tell attendees about your organization

How to Choose the Type of Event to Host

Now that you have an overview of the numerous options, how do you decide which is best for your organization? While there are no one-size-fits-all answers, here are a few things you can look at to help you decide:

Does your organization lend itself better to one type of event than another?

You don't have to be an organization whose mission involves health and wellness to host an athletic event, but if your focus is related, a 5K run/walk may be a good fit. When you look at the types of events available, consider what your organization does and the type of people who are in your database. If the average person on your list is unlikely to be able to pay $100 or more for a gala ticket, consider an event with a smaller ticket price. The same goes for your potential sponsor base: Who are your vendors or providers? Do any of them fit into a category that seems like a good match for a particular type of event? For example, an insurance company may be a great sponsor for a health fair. If your organization recovers food from local restaurants and hotels, perhaps a food and beverage event or cooking demonstration is the best match for you.

How much cash do you have available?

Some types of events definitely take more of an upfront cash outlay than others. Food and beverage events typically require a 25 to 50 percent deposit for the venue and other necessities, while other types of events may require few, if any, deposits. Be sure to get a true sense of what money can be used before event expenses come in, especially if it's a first-time event and you are unsure what sponsors and ticket sales you can expect.

How much staff do you have available?

While all events are time-consuming, some are more so than others. A food and beverage event with a hotel for both the venue and food and beverage takes much less time to organize than a tasting event, which may have 15-50 restaurants participating. Carefully think through who on your staff will manage the event and what time he or she has to put into it. Also consider what else that colleague could accomplish with that same amount of time. If your major gifts officer is spending 80 percent of her time on event planning, is the outcome going to net more revenue than if that person spent all her time soliciting major gifts? Carefully consider both the revenue potential, as well as the event's ability to solicit new supporters and increase the commitment of existing ones.

How many volunteers do you have and how engaged are they?

What does your "bench strength" look like? Volunteers can play crucial roles in event planning and thus ease the demands on your staff. But how active is your volunteer base? Are they really engaged and working? Or are they up for only a two-hour shift now and then? Do you have people with connections or sales ability who can help you line up new sponsors and auction items? Do you have enough people for event-day roles? Once you've chosen what type of event, also consider what components you want. For example, if your volunteer staff is new or not active, it may be better to skip the silent auction until you build up more help.

Who are your volunteers?

Even if you have a robust volunteer list, what type of people are they? Are they your community's social influencers? The type of people who will invite friends to a gala dinner—and most will attend? Are they connected to local businesses or others who tend to be charitable? Or are they better at plowing through a list of tasks? No matter what your volunteer profile is, there typically is a place where everyone can plug in, but it's important to consider the type of help you can get when choosing the type of event to host.

What do your contact lists look like?

How are you going to get people to your event? Your database may be a good indicator of what type of event you should choose. Is your list small? (See Chapter 1.) Are they typically unresponsive when you send messages to them?

Is it high non-open rates or just lack of response once a message has been opened? Or does your outreach have good open rates and responses? If your list is smaller or less responsive than you want, events with smaller ticket prices and broader appeal make more sense—unless your volunteer base can help make up for your list's shortcomings.

How to Make Your Event Stand Out

Healthy attendance can go a long way toward a healthy financial return. Increased attendance means not only more ticket sales revenue, but also more people to bid on auction items, make donations and bring the event more marketing power when selling to potential sponsors. So what can you do to help boost those numbers? Here are a few things to consider:

The date

Does your gala fall on the same night as another big one in town? Is your 5K competing with another nearby race—and does that one boast a flatter course or better swag? Before solidifying the date, do some online research. If you know of another event that is similar to yours and is typically around the same time of year, don't be afraid to call the sponsoring organization to be sure your events aren't happening on the same date.

Something different

How can you make your event distinctive? If you're organizing a race, can you select or add a less common distance, perhaps 10K or one mile? Some special treat for kids? Often there are several 5K's on a Saturday morning, so what can you provide to make someone choose yours? Or maybe even drive an extra 10 or 15 minutes to attend your event instead of one closer to home? Same for golf tournaments. Can you add a distinctive contest? An unusual or coveted prize such as a high-end set of golf clubs? Can your gala be themed in a way that is more fun, perhaps featuring costumes or something interactive? Anything you can do to make your event stand out should help you increase attendance and possibly attract media attention.

Star power

A celebrity, national or more likely local, can go a long way to build attendance. Food-and-wine events with your city's favorite chefs, athletic events with local TV or radio personalities or galas with a star speaker can really push your event into the spotlight. How do you find a local celebrity? This is where it really pays to tap into your board of directors and volunteer base to see who they know. Tell them you'd love to have someone with star power at the event and brainstorm their connections to see if you can get the opportunity to tell the celebrity about your organization. When meeting with potential media sponsors, ask them if one of their personalities could become part of your event.

Even if you don't have star power or something unique, try to at least incorporate a feature that makes your event different from last year's. It can be the menu, décor, color scheme or something smaller, but you want returning guests to feel that the event is fresh. Tap into the creative people on your staff or committees as you plan to keep things exciting. Creativity will help make your event stand out both from other events as well as in the minds of your repeat attendees.

CHAPTER TO-DO LIST

✔ **Review type of events check list and choose which one to host.**

✔ **Brainstorm ways to make your event stand out.**

Section Two

Event Fundraising Revenue Streams

To get your FREE copy of the A-to-Z Guide to Event Fundraising appendix
full of useful tools, checklists, sample document and worksheets, visit
docs.AtoZEventFundraising.com.

CHAPTER

3

SPONSORSHIPS

In This Chapter

- ✔ **Sponsorship overview**
- ✔ **How to build a sponsor prospect list**
- ✔ **Creating a sponsor package**
- ✔ **How to price sponsorships**
- ✔ **What to do once you have a sponsor**

The Basics

Sponsorships can be one of the biggest sources of revenue for your event. Solicited early in the planning process, sponsorships can be not only the insurance policy your event needs to be sure you end up in the black, but they also can bring in new supporters. Below are the most common questions about event sponsorships.

What is it?

A **sponsorship** is a monetary donation that helps pay the expenses of an event. The sponsor can be a large or small company, or even an individual (called a **patron**). Sponsorships can also be **in-kind**. (See Chapter 7.) When deciding your sponsorship goal, aim for at least the amount you need to cover the direct costs of the event, such as venue, entertainment and food and beverage.

sponsorship: financial support received from a company or individual to support a special event

patrons: individuals who sponsor an event

in-kind sponsorship: a donation of goods or services, instead of cash, in payment for their sponsorship

Who typically buys an event sponsorship?

The best prospects are companies:

- located near the event, especially those that are consumer-based (e.g., a clothing store, a chiropractor or restaurant),

- owned by members of the organization putting on the event (This works well with civic organizations such as Rotary or Kiwanis.),

- eager to market to the typical event attendee (e.g., a running store for a 5K),

- that have a history of supporting organizations with a cause similar to yours, or

- that are vendors to your organization, the people it serves or its volunteers/board members (e.g., a medical supply company for a health clinic).

Individuals willing to be sponsors tend to be those who are affiliated with your organization (perhaps a parent whose child benefits from your services) or who already support your organization or similar causes.

To create a sponsorship prospect list, brainstorm with staff members, committee members, board members and others helping with the event. Use the ideas above as a starting point, and when your list is complete, assign someone to solicit each prospect and determine a way to report progress. As in most sales processes, you will likely need ten prospects to find three that are interested before one will actually buy. Sponsorship sales is definitely a numbers game, but you should also work smart and pursue warm leads first. Ten targeted phone calls to people or companies you have relationships with are likely to be far more productive than a group email to 1,000 people you don't know.

What do you need to sell sponsorships?

Once you have assembled your prospect list, you will need a sponsor proposal, often called a **sponsor deck**. It includes information about the event and your organization, the different sponsorships levels available, and the price and benefits of each level. Later in this chapter is an example of a sponsor deck for a 5K race as well as information on how to build one for your event.

sponsor deck: a document given to potential sponsors that contains information about your event, a list of sponsor levels and the corresponding price and benefits at each level

Who should sell sponsorships?

The short answer is anyone who is willing and who you think has the skills to succeed. Most often, sponsorships are sold by organizational staff, higher-level committee members (event chairs, sponsorship chair, etc.) and board members. You can help both your staff and non-staff members be more successful by giving them the tools they need, including the sponsor deck, talking points, most commonly asked questions and answers, and stories about the impact your organization has had on those you help. (See Chapter 11.) Providing training, including role playing, and offering to attend meetings or conference calls with important potential sponsors can go a long way toward building confidence and success when selling event sponsorships.

When should you start selling sponsorships?

Once you have set most of the event details (date, location, etc.), you should begin selling sponsorships. It is important to keep in mind budgeting seasons, especially when selling to businesses. Companies often budget their marketing and charitable giving one to two months prior to the end of their fiscal year— and that could be a year before your event. But many companies set aside money for unforeseen opportunities, so you might get lucky. Even if it's too late for this year's event, your inquiry serves as an introduction and sets the stage for a potential sponsorship next year. If there is interest, you may want to extend complimentary tickets to attend this year's event in hopes that they will sponsor the following year.

How to Build a Sponsor Deck

Sponsor decks are the menu of opportunities available to companies and patrons interested in supporting your event. In the rest of this chapter, we will explore how to build a sponsor deck to increase sponsorship revenue at your event.

Sponsor Deck Levels

Sponsor decks contain a list of levels that have a name (e.g., Platinum, Gold or Bronze), benefits the sponsor receives at each of those levels and a price for each. Sponsor decks can have as few as two levels, but many have a dozen or more. When listing your levels, the highest dollar amount (and coinciding benefits) should be at the top with less expensive levels below. If you have any specialty sponsorships (more on these below), list them below your basic levels. The following sponsor deck, for a 5K walk/run, features six levels and two specialty sponsorships.

SPONSORSHIP OPPORTUNITIES FOR YOUR ORGANIZATION'S 5K WALK/RUN	
Presenting (or Co-Presenting)	
• Presenting-level event recognition including "presented by" with logo on all race communications, such as print media, signs, race shirt, website and social media • Verbal recognition on race day • 2 tables at the race-day expo • 25 race entries, including number, race shirt & goody bag • Personalized sponsor wall plaque • Limit of two sponsors at this level	$5,000
Platinum	
• Logo recognition on signs, print media, race shirt, website and social media • Verbal recognition on race day • 1 table at the race day expo • 10 race entries, including number, shirt & goody bag • Personalized sponsor wall plaque	$2,500
Gold	
• Logo recognition on signs, race shirt, print media, website and social media • Verbal recognition on race day • 1 table at the race day expo • 5 race entries, including number, race shirt & goody bag • Personalized sponsor wall plaque	$1,500

Silver	
• Name recognition on signs, race shirt, print media, website and social media • Verbal recognition on race day • 2 race entries, including number, race shirt & goody bag • Personalized sponsor wall plaque	$1,000
Bronze	
• Name recognition on signs • 1 race entry, including number, race shirt & goody bag • Personalized sponsor wall plaque	$ 500
Friend (individuals only)	
• 1 race entry, including number, race shirt & goody bag	$ 250
ADDITIONAL SPONSORSHIPS	
Tech Race Shirt Sponsor	
• Name recognition, as race shirt sponsor, both on signs and on race shirt • 2 official race shirts • 1 race entry, including number, race shirt & goody bag	$1,000
Water Table Sponsor	
• Name recognition, as race water table sponsor, both on signs and on race shirt • 1 race entry, including number, race shirt & goody bag	$500

How do you know how many levels to offer? There is no correct or incorrect number, but for new events you likely want it to be similar to the one above. As your event gathers momentum or you add components, you may want to expand it by adding new levels or some of the specialty opportunities listed below.

When choosing the benefits at each level, think about the potential sponsors. In this example, a sponsor wall plaque is included because the sponsors are likely to be small community businesses and will probably value showing customers their active role in the community. If you are working with larger corporate sponsors, or individuals, this benefit may be an unneeded expense. Sponsor benefits should be things your sponsor wants, but make sure that they don't cost you more than the sponsor contributes.

Some potential sponsor benefits are:

- Tickets or participant registrations

- Logo (for higher sponsors) or name (for lower sponsors) on event materials such as marketing flyers, signage, tickets, A/V presentation

- Logo, name or advertisement in program. If you give program advertisements as a benefit, check your tax laws. **TIP** Normal advertisements for products or services (versus an ad that says "XYZ Company is proud to support ABC Organization") can be considered unrelated business income (UBI) which may cause tax implications for your organization. A safe bet is to require your program ads to focus on supporting your organization, versus the sale of a product or service.

- Logo or name on event advertising

- Logo or name on event or organization's website

- Name in organization's annual report

- Social media mentions

- Plaque or gift

- Verbal recognition from stage

- Table or expo space to promote product or company

- Opportunity to place item in gift or goody bags

Naming sponsor levels Platinum through Bronze is common, but you may want to be more creative. The names can theme around either your event or your organization. A casino party could be Blackjack, Poker, Roulette. Events that have a military tie-in could be General, Colonel, Major, etc. Try to create a hierarchy that makes sense; for example, the "General" level costs more than "Lieutenant." This can be a great way for a creative person on your staff or committee to have fun!

Specialty Sponsorship Opportunities

Offering a handful of specialty sponsorships is often a good way to provide companies with additional marketing. Examples include a T-shirt for a 5K race and a wine glass at a food and beverage event. If your event needs these items, selling a sponsorship for the item and printing the sponsor's logo on the item not only gives your sponsor additional marketing value (as people wear the logo on their back or hold the glass all night), it can cover the cost of an essential item.

When thinking about these opportunities, look at your expenses and see if any of them might have marketing appeal. Some ideas are below:

Type of Event	Potential Sponsor Opportunities
Athletic Events	• T-shirt or golf shirt • Pre-party (either day of event or prior) • After-party/ 19th Hole • Golf ball or golf tee • Hole-in-one • Water and/or water table • Tot trot (or children's race) – great for a business that focuses on children • Signs* • Door prize* • Media*
Food and Beverage Events	• Wine and/or champagne glass • Champagne toast • VIP party (or area) • Reception/cocktail hour • After-party • Patron party • Ticket • Parking (or valet parking) • Table • Course (for seated dinner) • Auction paddle • Area of event (stage, registration, VIP, florals, etc.) • Volunteer or guest gift • Gift bag (Typically this sponsorship is for the bag itself, not what is inside.) • Product* • Photo booth • Automotive [usually to display car(s) at the event] • Auction • Door prize* • Signs* • Media* • Photographer/Videographer
Other Events	• Catwalk (fashion shows) • Blood pressure screening (for health fairs) • Tent sponsor (outdoor events)

* Possible in-kind sponsorships (See Chapter 7.)

Real World Example:

A luxury kitchen appliance company wanted to introduce its newest product to food-and-wine festival attendees. To accommodate the sponsors, organizers created a "Stage Sponsor" that included the benefit of recruiting local and esteemed chefs to do cooking demonstrations using the sponsor company's appliances throughout the event.

Offer just a few specialty sponsorships on your deck so that it doesn't become overwhelming. It's smart to have a couple other options to share with those soliciting sponsors. When meeting with potential sponsors, ask them what they are looking for and consider creating specialty sponsorships based on their needs. This creates a win-win opportunity for you and the sponsor.

How to Price Sponsorships

By now you are likely asking: "How do I know how to price sponsorships?" There are multiple components that go into sponsor-level pricing, and although there is no simple equation for knowing where to start your top level, here are some considerations:

History of your event

Events that have been around longer or have shown a track record of success can garner higher sponsorship levels.

How established and well regarded your organization is

The older, better-known and highly regarded your organization is, the more likely you can charge higher rates.

Number of participants

Events that have large turnouts usually provide a sponsor with more marketing reach, and can have higher rates.

Media partnerships

Media sponsorships, which are typically in-kind, may include print or online advertisements in local, regional or national newspapers, magazines or TV. These media partnerships can exponentially increase your sponsorship potential. An ad with a logo in a local magazine with a circulation of 5,000 could mean ten times the eye views for a 5K that typically has 500 runners. (See Chapter 10.)

Celebrity component

Your event can be significantly more attractive to a sponsor if you can line up a national or local celebrity as an honorary chairperson, host committee member (especially if you can use the person's name in your promotional materials), leader for your race or even as an emcee.

What other events are in your city?

Having a one-of-a-kind event, choosing a date or time of year that is not event-heavy, or having an audience that is typically difficult to market to increases your chances of signing up sponsors and maximizing the amounts they are willing to contribute. Even with a good evaluation of your event using the criteria above, it can still be difficult to decide whether your highest level should be $50,000 or $100,000. Or for smaller events, $1,000 or $1,500. Don't be afraid to check out your competition. If another organization is doing a similar event, looking at the sponsorship levels may help you decide what range you should offer.

Whatever you decide, put in an "aspiration" sponsor level, or one a bit higher than you think is possible to sell. Potential sponsors often look at a sponsor deck the same way a person reads a wine menu. They look at the most expensive, then the least expensive, and most often choose an offering in between. It may be unlikely that you get that highest level initially, but it is still great to have it on your sponsor deck and one day, as your event continues to grow and have success, you will get a buyer!

Real World Example:

A food and beverage event had a sponsor deck with a total of ten levels and specialty opportunities. A local philanthropist committed to sponsoring the event, but before choosing a level, asked which was the highest. She purposefully chose one level down from the highest one offered as she didn't want to look like the main sponsor of the event. Had an aspiration level not been included, the event would have raised $10,000 less.

Pricing specialty sponsorships

For some specialty sponsorships, your organization will be responsible for ordering an item with the sponsor's logo on it, such as a wine glass or gift bag. If so, the price of the sponsorship should include both the cost of the customized item and additional profit for the event. If you need to buy the item whether you get a sponsor or not, covering the cost (or even partial cost) would still help you offset some of your expenses. (See Chapter 7.)

Real World Example:

A company was interested in the wine glass sponsorship at a seated dinner. Here's how the organization decided how to price the sponsorship:

Cost to rent wine glasses = $1,000

Cost to purchase wine glasses with logo (including shipping, breakage, washing) = $2,000

Break-even wine glass sponsorship price: $2,000 for glasses - $1,000 sponsorship = $1,000 (same cost as rental)

The sponsorship was offered at $3,000. The sponsor asked to negotiate, finally giving $2,500, which netted the event $1,500 more than had the sponsorship not been offered.

In addition, some sponsors may want a completely customized sponsorship. Often called activations, these sponsorships should be priced similar to the example above to make sure you cover any additional costs that the activation required, and to ensure that there is net income for your organization. The larger the activation, the higher it should be priced.

What Else Should Be in a Sponsor Proposal?

Sponsor proposals should be your sales presentation in one neat package. When possible, the proposal and corresponding deck should be presented by a trained staff member or volunteer who can learn about the potential sponsor's wants and needs so the best fit can be found. But if not, the deck should also be able to stand alone and answer most, if not all, of your potential sponsors' questions. Here is what your sponsor proposal should include:

Mandatory

- An overview of both your organization and the event

- Specifics about the event (where, when, time, ticket or participant price, special guests, any other details). If you don't have 100 percent of these details finalized, you can still create a sponsor proposal with a handful of TBD's, but not too many!

- Impact of your organization and, if possible, what last year's event was able to do in the community (See Chapter 11.)

- Sponsor deck with levels, benefits and prices

- Sponsorship commitment/agreement form

Nice to have

- List of past sponsors or supporters (honorary chairs, guests of honor, etc.)

- Demographics of attendees

- Photos from past events

- Media that is confirmed (If logos will be included in ads, that information should also be in the sponsor benefits details.)

- Media clips from previous year

Sponsor proposals should be in both hard copy and electronic form. The electronic form should be a non-editable PDF that can be easily emailed to both those who are helping you sell the sponsorships, as well as to potential sponsors. You also will likely need a print version of the sponsor deck for in-person meetings. One word of caution: While it's impressive to have a fancy sponsor proposal, most sponsors would prefer a simpler, less expensive presentation demonstrating that you keep fundraising expenses low so you have more to devote to your mission.

TIP

Sponsor Commitments and Payments

It is important to have documentation, such as an agreement that confirms the sponsor's commitment to the event. The agreement should contain all the important event information (date, location, etc.) as well as the sponsor's level, financial commitment and the benefits the sponsor will receive. Be sure to include deadlines for receiving both the agreement and payment in order to get sponsor benefits (i.e. a commitment and payment must be received by XX/XX/XX in order to have sponsor logo placed on signage and race T-shirt).

Once you have received an agreement, send an invoice with the payment due dates. Some companies will make a payment from the agreement, but sending an invoice often helps you get the money more quickly and alleviates some of the stress of tracking down missing payments close to event day. While most sponsors meet the deadline, it can help to deliver some of the benefits (e.g., tickets, race numbers) only after payment has been received. If you choose to do this, be sure to clearly state that information in the sponsor commitment form.

TIP

I've got a sponsor. Now what?

You've got a sponsor committed to your event, and you've received the agreement and sent an invoice. What's next? One of your most important jobs is to ensure that your sponsors receive everything they have been promised. Whether this is a full-page ad in the program, a logo on a race T-shirt or a larger deliverable (often called an activation), it is important to set up systems to be sure that each sponsor receives all the benefits for the level selected.

A great way to keep track of the details is to use a spreadsheet with columns for sponsor name, address, contact information, level and amount of sponsorship. It can also include a column for each sponsor benefit, such as tickets, race numbers, whether they get a booth or table, etc.

For example, if logo placement in a local newspaper ad is a benefit, create yes/no columns titled "received logo" and "logo in ad." That will make it easier to see which logos you either need to get or are missing when proofing the advertisement. No matter what sponsor benefits you are providing, always ask someone to look at your worksheet and reproof any items with sponsor logos to make sure you haven't forgotten anyone. A fresh set of eyes will often pick up things you may miss after looking at the same information countless times. If the ad is published without the logo, you are going to have an unhappy conversation with the sponsor—and it may be the last time that company is a sponsor.

If you like all your information in one place, create a master spreadsheet with the sponsor worksheet as one of the pages. An **TIP** Excel document works well because not only can you keep track of the many different components on separate worksheets (sponsors, tickets, auction items, program details, etc.), you can also create a summary worksheet that pulls data from other worksheets, thus giving you an "at a glance" look at your event.

A sample editable master spreadsheet can be found in the downloadable appendix at docs.AtoZEventFundraising.com.

Aside from ensuring that your sponsors receive everything they are entitled to, it is important to connect with them so they will maintain or even enhance their engagement with your organization. Some good ways to do this are: 1) Greet them in person when they arrive at the event (or ask another committee member to do so), 2) Arrange for them to meet people touched by your organization's work, either at the event or at another time, and 3) Keep them informed about your organization and its accomplishments.

CHAPTER TO-DO LIST

✔ **Brainstorm to create, or add to, a sponsor prospect list.**

✔ **For first-time events, research similar events to determine average sponsor pricing and benefits.**

✔ **Create a sponsor proposal, including sponsor deck.**

✔ **Train staff, committee and/or board members to sell sponsorships. Sell sponsorships.**

✔ **Track sponsorships, payments and benefits to ensure all deliverables are met.**

To get your FREE downloadable Sample Master Spreadsheet, visit **docs.AtoZEventFundraising.com.**

TICKET SALES & PARTICIPANT FEES

In This Chapter

- ✔ Ticket sales or participation fees overview

- ✔ How to raise revenue from ticket sales or participation fees

- ✔ How to price your tickets

- ✔ How to determine how many tickets to sell

- ✔ How to maximize ticket sales

- ✔ Other common questions about tickets

The Basics

The second-most common source of revenue from an event fundraiser is the money people pay to attend. Below are the most common questions about this revenue stream.

What is it?

Whether it's a ticket to your talent show or seated dinner, entry fees for a walk/run or registration fees for your golf tournament, maximizing turnout for your event not only brings in revenue for your organization; it also delivers increased marketing power for sponsors and

ticket sales or participant fees: revenue raised from selling tickets or paid registrations for events

greater opportunity to raise more funds at the event, perhaps at an auction. (For ease of understanding, any type of revenue from **ticket sales or participant fees** will be called a "ticket" in this chapter.)

What do you need?

Needs vary, depending on the type of event. You may need a paper ticket or wristband to give each person who purchases a ticket. Or, a confirmation email may fit the bill. In addition, you need a method to keep track of ticket sales. Many times, an online sales tool is helpful (e.g., Active.com for an athletic event), but for less-complex events, that may not be necessary.

Who should sell the tickets?

Everyone! A ticket sales committee, overall committee members, board members and staff should all have ticket sales responsibilities.

When should you start?

It's almost never too early to begin informing people about your event and selling tickets. Once you have finalized the event details (date, location, etc.), you should post information in numerous and varied locations. You may want to send a "save the date" email or postcard or post it to your website or online community calendars.

Who will buy tickets?

Depending on the type of event, a wide variety of people may purchase tickets. Past supporters (donors, volunteers, people who have received your program's services, etc.) are prime candidates. In addition, enthusiasts for the type of event (e.g., runners for a 5K or foodies for a tasting event) are potential buyers.

How to Price Your Tickets

Determining a ticket price can feel overwhelming. Here are a few considerations:

What do you need to spend on each attendee?

If you are organizing a 5K, what will it cost to provide a T-shirt, race number, water stands and other items, based on the anticipated number of participants? If it's a seated dinner, what will food and beverage cost per person along with her portion of the overall event expenses (rentals, décor, entertainment, etc)? If you are using an online service to sell tickets, factor those costs in as well. If possible, these hard costs should at least be covered by your ticket price.

If it's a repeat event, how were your ticket sales last year?

If your attendance was less than you anticipated, do you think the price of the ticket had something to do with it?

What do similar events charge?

Most towns have a "going rate" for certain types of events. Do a bit of research to see what other organizations are charging for similar events and use that information to help guide your decisions.

Should you have different ticket levels?

A varied pricing structure often helps raise additional revenue or encourages earlier ticket sales (an early-registration discount). If you offer a VIP ticket at a premium price, those attendees should receive an additional benefit. It could be a hat at a 5K, early admission, a VIP area with exclusive food and drinks, a gift bag (or premium gift bag if everyone is getting a bag) or a special experience. Another option is a "friends and family" discount, offered either from the beginning or closer to the event date if sales are lagging.

Deciding How Many Tickets to Sell

When determining how many tickets to sell, consider the following:

Does the venue have a limited capacity?

It is important to discuss such limits with the person who manages the venue. If you're having a seated dinner, how many tables of 8 or 10 can you fit comfortably along with everything else you need to set up (e.g., entertainment stage, silent auction tables, VIP area, check in areas, coat check). If it's a tasting event, how many people can roam around comfortably with the set-up you are planning? For a golf tournament, how many foursomes can play in the time you are allotting? Do the police or other authorities set maximums for a run/walk? Does allowing an additional

50 runners force you to rent more port-a-potties and thus turn your would-be money-maker into a money-loser? Or does selling more tickets make the event so crowded that guests will think twice about returning next year? This is especially important with outdoor events because if the weather is bad, all guests will have to squeeze under a tent instead of wandering around in open areas.

Don't forget your sponsors, special guests and potential new sponsors or donors.

If you must limit the number of attendees, it is important to subtract the number of tickets you need for both committed and anticipated sponsors, special guests (e.g., honorary chairs), committee members, potential board members or sponsors, large donors, media, etc. before determining the number you can sell. It is also typical during the final days before the event for people to ask for last-minute tickets. Some are sure to be people you simply can't turn down, so plan a small buffer.

Should you oversell?

Most likely, yes. Even the most prestigious event will have a few no-shows. How many can you oversell by? That depends. How tight is your capacity restriction? A seated dinner where literally it's impossible to fit in another guest will have less room for overselling than a 5K or tasting event. What is the worst thing that can happen if you are oversold? Will the fire code force you to shut down the event or refuse entry? Or is it just a bit more crowded than you had planned? Will you run out of food? The potential consequences of an oversold event should be weighed before deciding your margin of error.

How to Maximize Ticket Sales

Here are a few strategies for selling out your events.

Save the date.

Once your event details are determined, send your organizational supporters information about the event so they can put it on their calendar. If possible, also provide a way to purchase tickets. Everyone is busy, so the sooner you can get your event etched into your supporters' schedules, the better.

Set goals.

Set ticket sales goal, either overall or per person, and ask your committee, board members and staff to help reach that goal.

Consider creating a ticket sales incentive program.

Some organizations have success with a ticket incentive program, which rewards those who sell a lot of tickets. For example, a person receives a free ticket for every 10 she sells. Another approach is to designate table captains, which each one receiving a free ticket if they sell the remaining seats at their table.

Make it easy to purchase.

If tickets are available online, make it easy to get to the page by creating a simple, easy to remember web address and keep the number of steps to purchase to a minimum. If using paper order forms, these too should be brief. Return phone calls promptly.

List your event on local websites.

Most cities have websites that allow you to list local events. They include Patch.com, Yelp and the local newspaper. Most do not charge for the listing, but it can be time-consuming as many require you to set up accounts. That makes this a great job for a volunteer or intern. (See Chapter 10.)

Real World Example:

A 5K race encouraged people to register as a team and extended outreach to local schools and businesses. Any team that had at least 15 runners registered by four weeks prior to the race got the team name on the race T-shirt. The efforts were a success, with teams making up 20 percent of the runners.

Don't underestimate the power of a team.

Athletic events—and almost any other event—are more fun when you attend with a group. Encourage the idea of friends, family and co-workers joining together. Many online sites offer this option, or you can send a follow-up email to current registrants asking them to invite a friend. This can be a great way to boost turnout.

More Common Questions about Ticket Sales

Here are a few other things to consider about tickets:

Should you give away tickets?

In some situations, it may be advantageous to give complimentary tickets, even though it means a loss of revenue. It's a good opportunity to thank and steward an existing donor, cultivate potential donors or sponsors (especially if the impact piece of your event is strong, as explained in Chapter 11), and put potential auction bidders or donors in the room. Some organizations also give free tickets to committee members. If you have limited seating, it may not be prudent to give away tickets to all, or even some, committee members. On the other hand, it can be a good incentive for someone to chair a committee or for members to sell tickets. There is no right or wrong answer, but it is important that committee members know from the start of the planning process what is expected. A friends-and-family discount is another option.

What if you haven't sold as many tickets as you'd hoped, and the event is getting close?

Ticket revenue is often the most difficult source to predict, for many reasons. For athletic events, 80 percent or more of your ticket sales will come in during the last two or three weeks. If weather cooperates, you can easily pick up another 10 to 20 percent on race day. For other types of events, especially those with a less expensive ticket, the same scenario is not uncommon. The more expensive and more formal the event, the less chance you will see a spike in last-minute sales. If sales are lagging, double up on marketing and PR efforts, consider offering a friends-and-family discount, or increase incentives for your committee. Keep the faith; you often see a spike in sales even when it appears dismal.

If ticket sales are too low, should I cancel?

What if your event is around the corner and you are almost sure you won't sell enough tickets to make the event a success? Should you cancel? It depends. If sponsorship sales have covered your expenses, you are likely better off moving forward with the event and potentially giving some tickets away, especially if you are planning to have the event again in subsequent years. The same is true if you feel confident that your expenses will be covered by auctions or donations the night of the event. But when you know the event is going to lose money and your organization really can't sustain the loss, give serious consideration to cancelling so you can at least shrink the loss. Be sure to carefully weigh all the consequences; you will have to return auction items, sponsors' donations, in-kind contributions, and anything else you received.

Are the tickets tax-deductible?

Typically, the ticket price, less the fair market value of the goods and services the purchaser receives, is considered the donation and is tax-deductible. That amount should be printed either on the ticket or on the receipt. For example, if your event includes a glass of wine and hors d'oeuvres valued at $25 and the ticket price is $45, the tax-deductible portion would be $20.

Tie ticket price to organization impact.

A great way to boost sales is to tell would-be purchasers what the purchase amount can help your organization accomplish. For example, on the ticket and at the point or purchase, it could say: "Your $50 ticket can provide a homeless child diapers for a month." (See Chapter 11.)

Print tickets or not?

With so much technology, many events no longer print tickets. Here are a few pros and cons to consider when deciding whether you should print tickets or use another type of identification at entry to the event.

Printed Tickets	
PROS	• Entry to the event is easy. Show the ticket taker your ticket and walk in – no long lines at will-call or check-in. • For events with a lot of sponsors, tickets can be sent to one contact, who can pass them out to employees, customers, etc. easily. • For more expensive events, a ticket printed on high-quality paper can create increased perceived value. • It can be an effective way to gather attendee information. With a small form on the ticket (name, phone, email, perhaps organization if a business event), you can have a raffle and gather attendee information so you can cultivate them after the event. (See Chapter 12.) This is especially helpful if some tickets sold in groups or there are a lot of sponsor tickets so you don't have individual information. For an event that tends to have more individual purchasers (e.g., a 5K with online registration), this may not be needed.
CONS	• Printing and mailing tickets can be expensive and time-consuming. • At least some mailed tickets never reach the intended recipient (slow mail, misplaced on delivery, etc.), and you may have a last-minute flurry of people calling about missing tickets. Assign a committee or staff member to field these calls and emails.
No Printed Tickets	
PROS	• Cost of printing and mailing tickets is avoided. • As VIP guests arrive, staff can be on call to greet them and give them special attention (via notification from the people working the ticket entry area)
CONS	• Entry lines can be long and bothersome to the guests. • Gathering attendee information, if you don't already have it, can be more challenging, but not impossible. • Additional staff is needed at event entry to help move lines quickly.

Ticket sales can be one of the most stressful revenue streams, especially for athletic events when weather and other factors tend to keep people from committing until the last minute. Using some of the tactics listed above can help decrease the stress level and increase sales success.

Chapter To-Do List

✔ **Determine price of tickets or participant fees.**

✔ **For events with limited capacity, determine how many tickets to sell. Create a method of tracking ticket sales.**

✔ **Create a goal for the number of tickets to be sold and strategies for maximizing ticket sales, including marketing and PR efforts.**

✔ **Determine if you want to sell tickets online or use another method, as well as if you will be printing tickets.**

AUCTIONS

In This Chapter

✔ Auction overview

✔ Live auctions – best items to solicit and how to maximize revenue

✔ Hiring a professional auctioneer

✔ Silent auctions – best items to solicit, maximizing revenue, logistics and paperwork

✔ Choosing whether to use a technology-based auction system

✔ Online auctions

The Basics

Another way of earning revenue at an event is through an auction. Live and silent auctions are the most common. Whether you choose to offer just a handful of live auction items or an extensive silent auction, guests often love to shop, and this can significantly increase your revenue. Below are some common questions.

What is it?

An auction is the sale of items, services or experiences to your guests. A **live auction** features an auctioneer selling items in front of guests, who bid on the items they want by raising a paddle or their hand. At a **silent auction** guests bid via paper, smartphone or tablet on items until a specified ending time. An **online auction** allows guests to bid via the Internet, and has the flexibility of being open before, during and/or after the event. No matter which type of auction you offer, guests will bid on the items available, and the person with the highest bid when the auction closes wins the item. Your organization will receive the money that the winner pays.

live auction: sale of goods, services or experiences to the highest bidder where guests bid openly against one another "live" with the help of an auctioneer

silent auction: sale of goods, services or experiences to the highest bidder, either by writing bids on a paper bid sheet, smartphone or tablet

online auction: sale of goods, services or experiences to the highest bidder using the Internet to place bids

What do you need?

An auction solicitation letter, including information about your event, along with a follow-up phone call is an effective way to gather auction items. In addition, for larger auction donations, you may want to use your sponsor deck to make donors with a larger donation value in-kind event sponsors. Consider hiring a professional auctioneer and/or using an auction technology company to allow for bidding with a smartphone or tablet at the event. (See more about these later in the chapter.)

Who should solicit auction items?

Select anyone who is willing and who you think has the tools for the job. Unlike sponsorships, almost anyone can solicit auction donations from local businesses that you have gathered on a list. Or your solicitor can approach businesses that she frequents herself. Help your committee and volunteers by giving them the information they need, such as a solicitation letter, a form and scripts.

When should you start?

It's almost never too early to start soliciting auction items, but event sponsorship solicitations should come first. For larger donations, consider the budgeting season of potential donors.

Who will donate items, services or experiences?

Auction donors can come from a variety of places, and the list of prospects probably will resemble the one you used in seeking sponsors. Solicitations are typically more successful when someone has a relationship with the potential donor. Use the list below to brainstorm with staff members, committee members, board members and others helping with the event to create your contact list of businesses. Some popular businesses to approach are those that are:

- located near the event, especially those that are consumer-based (i.e., a clothing store or a chiropractor),

- owned by members of the organization putting on the event (This works well with civic organizations such as Rotary or Kiwanis.),

- want to market to the typical attendee (e.g., a running store for a 5K),

- have a history of supporting organizations with a cause similar to yours, and

- vendors to your organization, the people it serves or its volunteers/board members.

This list is the same as the one for sponsors. Some businesses lend themselves more towards one ot the other (e.g. a hair salon for auction), but if you are in doubt, ask for sponsorship first.

If you solicit a business for a cash sponsorship and get a no, you should immediately say, "I understand you can't help with a cash sponsorship, but can you support us by donating a product, service or gift certificate for our auction?"

How will you solicit items?

Items can be solicited in a variety of ways. Once a solicitation letter and form have been created, organizational staff, board members and committee members can ask businesses to donate goods either in person or via email. In addition, it is often helpful to create a mailing list of people to ask and to mail both the letter and auction commitment form to the list you've created. Letters should contain information about your event, your organization and how the funds will be used. The auction commitment form should ask for all the information you need both for the bid sheets, as well as sending an acknowledgment/thank you letter after the event.

Live Auctions

Live auctions feature the sale of items in front of event attendees with the help of an auctioneer. Typically, the items are the best ones that you have procured for the event, both in value and perceived quality. You often see trips, "can't buy" experiences and unusual or difficult-to-get items in live auctions. Auctioneers usually get attendees to bid more for items than they would in a silent auction, due to the additional attention it gets on stage and a bit of peer pressure.

When Should Your Event Have a Live Auction?

Live auctions are a good choice when you have some, if not most, of the following:

Ability to get the attention of enough guests at auction time

It is not necessary for all of your guests to pay attention for it be successful. You just need enough people who have the means to bid to be able to hear and participate. You do need to be able to alert interested guests that the auction is about to start, and if possible, provide seating so they are comfortable.

Have higher-value items, especially ones you typically can't buy

A live auction isn't a place for the local pet store's gift basket. A trip is great— but it's even better if you have a personalized chef dinner at a local restaurant to go with it. Tickets to an event with a special VIP experience are better than tickets you can easily get online.

A good sound system, lighting and a stage

A place for the auctioneer to stand that is visible and proper A/V are essentials. If your audience can't hear or see your auctioneer, it will be hard to bid!

Ability to market your live auction items sufficiently prior to the event

Be sure that guests know about the items you are offering. List them on the event page of your website, send an email to ticket purchasers prior to the event, have a display table with the items (or their descriptions), include the list in the program or handout and show items on A/V screens during the auction itself.

Live Auction Items

Live auctions can range from just a few items to dozens, but most have three to twelve. Again, a lot of this depends on what items you have of the right value and uniqueness to be in the live auction. It is best to start with one of the less-valuable items (either monetarily or perceived) and work up to the most valuable. Also, try not to group similar items together. If you are using a professional auctioneer, ask for her advice on the best order. These categories are ones that often sell the best.

Travel

Whether the destination is within driving distance or an international getaway, travel is often a winner in live auctions. If you want to boost the final price, include as many of the components of a complete trip as possible. Naturally, a trip that includes hotel, a custom tasting menu at an area restaurant, tickets to an event and airfare will sell for more than an item that has only airfare and hotel. If you have the right people in your audience, it may be worth paying for some of these items in order to provide a more complete package.

Experiences

People love to buy what isn't for sale. Examples include a local chef cooking dinner for 10 people in your home, a behind-the-scenes tour, lunch or coffee with a local celebrity or esteemed business person, your name as a character in a book written by a local author, a chance to drive a car at a local race track, or a chance to spend a day with a chef, sports team member, TV personality, etc. Things that are difficult to buy, like a ticket to a sold-out event, are also popular. Sports enthusiasts may enjoy a tour of a local team's locker room. Other ideas are casino parties, Oscar parties and a clam or oyster bake. When possible, expand the number of people your item is for to help increase the funds raised. A day at the spa for one is fun, but better for you and three girl-friends. Be careful though; a trip for 10 can be tough to coordinate. If you are offering trips for more than four, be sure to market the item as far in advance as possible so friends can plan ahead to bid.

Items

Seek items that are unusual or have a high retail value. Jewelry, artwork that is esteemed in your community and wine or spirits, especially hard-to-get bottles, large-format bottles or verticals (the same producer and varietal of wine, but several different vintages/years), are often successful. (Be sure to check any laws that pertain to selling alcoholic beverages in your city.) Know your audience, and be sure that your items will appeal to at least a handful of people who are attending and have the means to bid. If you are raising funds for your child's school, a painting that every child contributed to or the opportunity to be "principal for a day" may be very appealing. At a golf tournament, a golf cart could be a big winner.

It is important that potential bidders have a written description of the live auction items. It should include details about the item, its donor, and just as importantly, any exemptions, expiration dates or blackout periods (for example, ground transportation for a trip, gratuity on a dining experience). Think through what a buyer may assume is included and if it's not, be sure to list it in the fine print to protect your organization later if there is any question.

Do **not** provide retail values in the information the guests see at the event. Winning bids often exceed retail value (It's for charity you know!), but revealing the retail values ahead of time is like putting a stop light on the bidding.

Maximizing Revenue at your Live Auction

Once you have a great set of items to sell, you want to make sure that your auction makes as much money as possible. Here are a few tips.

Hold the auction as close to the impact portion of your event as possible

Time the auction as close as possible to when you tell your audience about your organization, the problem you are working to solve and your impact to date. The auction could start just after a guest speaker, a moving video or another type of presentation. Evoking emotion and showing your impact help increase the amount people bid tremendously. (See Chapter 11.) Also, start your live auction half to three-quarters of the way through the event. If you begin too early, guests may not be ready to listen; too late, and they may be out the door mentally or physically.

Real World Example:

At an event that benefitted summer camps for children with medical needs, a father who had four children who had attended the camp spoke passionately about how the camp provided a reprieve for his children. Not only was it fun, but it was a place where they could be "like everyone else" versus their normal feeling of being "different" due to frequent medical needs (testing, shots, etc.). He had the audience in tears. When he was done, attendees were ready to do whatever was needed to get every kid with these medical needs to this camp. Unfortunately, there was a 20-minute break before the auction started. By then, guests were mixing and mingling, and the attention was lost. Lesson: Don't wait!

Ensure ample bidding

Be sure you publicize your auction items prior to the event via email, your website or social media, as well as have the information displayed, printed and given to guests at the event. Tell your guests when the auction will begin by having ample signs throughout the venue with the start time, and remind people frequently with announcements. Some events even use attention-getters such as marching bands or volunteers walking with signs! You also want to be sure your guests can see, hear and ideally, be comfortable by providing seating or a suitable space to stand.

Another way to increase the likelihood of success is to "stock the pond" with bidders. Informing attendees about the items that will be offered and getting verbal commitments to bid should help. If you have complimentary tickets available, it usually helps to give tickets to past or potential bidders to be sure they attend. Your board or committee members, auctioneer, staff or other friends of the organization may have ideas about who to invite to increase the number and level of bids. These should be people actually willing to win—not "pretend" bidders whose role is to boost the offers. That tactic is considered unethical.

Arrange ahead of time to sell some items more than once, or up their value.

A common way to up the proceeds is to sell an item at the winning bid to the two top bidders. Once you have the first item sold once, you can offer it to the runner-up for the same amount, doubling your proceeds. (If he says no, you can offer it at his final bid.)

For this to be successful, make sure in advance that a second item is available. You can do this in a couple of ways. One is to ask the donor if she is willing to donate two if the bids reach a certain amount. Often this isn't possible, so you can ask if you can purchase the second one at a discount or at cost.

Another way to increase what an item will go for is to "up it" during the auction itself. For example, if you were giving away four tickets to an event, on stage you could bump it up to six. Sometimes a donor will do this unexpectedly, so it helps to have a volunteer paying attention to what is said on stage and make notes so you have all the information if there are any questions later.

Real World Example:

A trip for two to New York City was offered as a live auction item. It included first-class airfare, a two-night stay at a five-star hotel and a customized dinner for two at an esteemed restaurant, including a visit to your table from the chef. Prior to the event, the chef, who also served as an honorary chair of the event, agreed that if the item sold for at least $5,000, he would offer the dining portion to a second winner. The other items in the package were not donated a second time, but they could be purchased for an additional $4,000. The night of the event, the item sold for $8,000. The runner-up purchased the item for $7,500, bringing net revenue for the item to $11,500.

As much as possible, you should map out which items you may be able to sell twice or bump up before the event, and document if there is a minimum bid in order for the offer to be made. Make sure your auctioneer has all this information in his note cards or whatever form of communication you are using to let him know about the auction lots. These conversations should happen prior to the event so that the donor doesn't feel blindsided at the event by your extra request, making her less likely to donate in the future. No matter what, do not broadcast that the item will be sold twice prior to the event. In most cases, it's something you and the auctioneer discuss and use only if the bidding hits a set threshold.

Real World Example:

A private dinner with wine pairings was offered during a live auction and quickly hit $8,000. On stage, the auctioneer quietly asked the chef if he would consider donating twice since it was raising so much money. The chef said no, but after the event the organizers learned the reason he declined was his concern about the additional expense of the second winners' food-and-wine, less than $2,000. If the organizers had planned ahead and let the chef know that they would pay the additional expense on the second dinner, they would have made an additional $6,000. This is a good lesson in planning ahead for every item so you don't miss out on potential revenue.

Using companies for auction items on consignment

There are numerous companies that offer both live and silent auction items at no risk to organizations. This is called **consignment**. As your event gets established, you will likely receive phone calls and emails from them, but if you don't, an Internet search can help you find them. Typically, they give you the items prior to your event and if they sell, you pay them a predetermined amount. If it sells for more, you keep the difference. If they don't sell, you just return the items, and there is no cost to you. The positive side of this is that procuring items is easy. You, staff members, board members or committee members don't need to chase down items. Another positive is that you can often get items that are nearly impossible to get donated and often difficult even to buy. (Think Super Bowl tickets.) The downside is that it's not sure profit; if you can't get the minimum bid, you make nothing and thus waste an auction item. But it doesn't have to be an either-or situation. You can solicit items, and if you don't have enough, or enough with a "wow" factor, you can supplement them with items from an auction company.

> *consignment*: sale of goods, services or experiences that have been given to an organization without purchasing them in advance. A minimum bid must be reached and is paid to the consignment company. Anything in excess of the minimum bid is profit to the organization.

Auctioneers

Hiring a professional auctioneer (or better yet, getting one to donate his or her services) can be a game-changer in making your live auction a success. Professional auctioneers are entertaining, and they know how get the most money possible for your items. Persuading auctioneers to donate their services can be difficult, as it is often their main way of making a living. Then the question becomes: Is he worth the cost of their fee and potentially travel expenses?

Yes—if you have both the right combination of items and an audience with the means to bid on them. But how do you know? One way is to compare the cost of the auctioneer to the retail value of your auction items. Since you hope to get at least retail value for each one, if your items don't add up to significantly more than your auctioneer's fee, you probably should do without one.

Other things to consider: For repeat events, are your typical bidders attending? Do you have some new people likely to bid? Do you have items similar to those that have sold well in the past? The more yes's you answer to these questions, the more likely the auctioneer is worth the investment.

Whether you choose to have a professional or amateur auctioneer, there are a few things that will help her succeed:

- Place spotters (usually volunteers) in the audience to point out bidders to the auctioneer and help ensure that your auctioneer doesn't miss anyone.

- Give the auctioneer an information sheet or notecards with the details about each item. Be sure to include not only the details (how many people, how many nights, whether it is one of a kind, includes delivery, etc.) but also anything that makes your item unusual.

- Be sure your auctioneer is aware of the retail value of each item and if there are any minimum bids required (sometimes called a "reserve" or "consignment amount").

- Don't give her a script of exactly what to say, but do provide information about your organization. Focus on impact information (e.g., $500 will provide XX), talking points about your organization and what the funds raised will help accomplish. If you use an amateur, ask if he prefers a script or talking points.

Discuss with your auctioneer ahead of time what works best for her. Does she want a handheld microphone? Does she like a "catwalk" on the stage, if room allows, to get closer to bidders? It is also helpful to discuss the final auction items prior to the event and ask her opinion on the best order for the items. (Some auctioneers will charge an additional fee for this service.)

After "Going Once, Going Twice... Sold!"

Now that your item is sold, how should you go about collecting payment and delivering the item? Since most live auction items are big-ticket, it's best to collect the money as soon as possible. A staff member, volunteer or auction company representative should go to the guest once the sale is final with a mobile device (i.e., a tablet with a credit card processing application) to collect payment. Or, you can ask the winner to pay at a station set up for collection, preferably very close to the auction location.

You can also provide numbered auction paddles to guests who register their name and credit card information. This can be done with auction software or on paper. (Just be sure to properly handle sensitive credit card information.) It is still recommended that winners either sign for their transaction while at the event via a mobile device credit card processor, or on paper, so that you have proof of both the purchase and the amount paid.

Prompt and efficient delivery of the item helps the recipient feel happy about the auction and your organization. Every winner of an experience should receive a certificate listing the specifics of what he won, including expiration dates and exclusions, and the name and contact information for how to arrange the experience. If he purchased an item, give it to him when he pays or offer to present it at the end of the event. (If the item is large, offer to have a volunteer help bring it to the car.) If it's too big for immediate delivery, arrange for the winner to either pick it up or have it delivered at the time of payment. If delivery has an additional cost and the winner is responsible for it, spell that out in the item description so there are no surprises at checkout. If it's a big enough ticket item, you may want to include delivery, at least within a certain distance.

A few final thoughts on live auctions. They can be tricky. Finding the right equation of how many items is enough to make money (but not so many that the audience loses interest), getting the right bidders in the room and creating the right amount of competition can be a complicated equation. But it is usually worth the risks because live auctions nearly always raise more money than the same items would in a silent auction. If you are new to live auctions, start small. Focus on soliciting the best-quality items possible and getting the bidders in the room. From there, you can build to a bigger and better one for future years.

Silent Auctions

Silent auctions take place during an event, with the items available for bidding via bid sheets or through smartphones. Silent auctions can feature only a handful of items or more than 100, usually in a variety of categories. Here are some common questions about silent auctions:

When Should You have a Silent Auction?

Silent auctions can raise a lot of money, but are labor-intensive. Aim to have at least a few of the following:

Ample space and lighting to display the items, as well as a guest flow that encourages bidding

Silent auctions take up space that otherwise might be used for seating or other aspects of the event. Be sure to factor this into your planning and decide if the revenue raised from the auction would be greater than potential ticket sales or another use for the same space.

People to solicit and pick up items

A silent auction is a time-consuming adventure no matter how well you plan, with a last-minute flurry of activity as you create bid sheets, display items and pick up the items. If you are already feeling uncertain that you have the volunteer or staff hours to put on a great event, a silent auction may not be for you.

An easy way for guests to pay

Accepting all payment types (credit cards, check or cash) is a necessity for most silent auctions. Fortunately, companies like Square or auction software companies make taking credit cards much easier. Be aware that some payment systems you may need access to power, phone lines or wireless internet, so do your research.

Silent Auction Items

The items that sell most quickly and for the most money are similar to those listed in the live auction section earlier in this chapter, but are typically worth less (either real or perceived). Best sellers include travel experiences (e.g., local hotel stays, drivable weekend getaways, destination events), experiences for two or more (e.g., sporting event tickets, food-and-wine events, shopping experiences, museum memberships), restaurant gift certificates, jewelry, wine or spirits, artwork and housewares. Again, know your audience. Think about your attendees and what they would likely want to buy.

There is no equation for deciding how many items you should have in your silent auction. It is important to put quality ahead of quantity because bidders can get auction fatigue if there are tables and tables of items. Look at the space for display and let your committee know how many items you will have room for and look to them to solicit the best items possible. If you do end up with a large number, you may want to create a "Super Silent" category featuring your best items in a prime spot. Highlight them in your marketing.

Too few items can also be a problem, especially if they have low value. If you do end up with only a handful of less-expensive items, you may want to consider a raffle instead. Guests can purchase raffle tickets and then place them in the jar of the items they would like to win. One winner is chosen from the ticket jar at the end of the event. (See Chapter 6.)

Maximizing Revenue at Your Silent Auction

Put the silent auction in high-traffic areas.

It is important to place your auction where guests will see it, especially if you are not using smartphone technology. Be sure to lead guests through or next to the auction on their way to where they want or need to go. For example, place auction tables on the way to the bar, guest tables or rest rooms. If that isn't possible, use signs and volunteers to not only let guests know where the auction is, but to encourage guests to look at what is available. If possible, place auction category signs high enough up that guests can see them across the room so they can easily find the ones they are interested in.

Ask for a minimum value when soliciting donations.

In theory, no matter what the price is for a donated item, it should help you raise more money for your organization. Even so, an item that doesn't draw a bid takes up valuable space, has wasted your staff or volunteer's time, and often cheapens the image of your auction, causing attendees to lose interest. A suggested minimum donation amount helps increase the quality of your auction. Depending on your event, it could be as low as $25 or as high as $250, or even more. Not all donors will adhere to your suggested minimum, but it often helps boost the value of the donated items. If you end up with items below the minimum, you can still use them, perhaps combining them with other items to create a larger-valued package.

Don't accept items that don't have a real value. For example: A portrait studio sends you a donation form for a "waived sitting fee" for a family portrait. Upon further investigation, you discover that the fee is <u>always</u> waived with a purchase of at least one photo. Without a donation of at least one picture, a polite decline of this item would be appropriate.

Determine where to start the bidding and select bid increments.

Bids can start at whatever amount you would like, typically a percentage of retail value (which should also be listed on the bid sheet or item description). The range of 30 to 50 percent is common for the starting bid. Bid increments are typically based on the item's overall value. For example, a necklace valued at $250 could have a starting bid of $125 along with $25 increments. An item with a $1,000 value might start at $500 with increments of $50, $75 or even $100. (Visit docs.AtoZGuidetoEventFundraising.com to download suggested bid increments based on item values.)

Package items.

Group items together to create one of higher value. A great example would be a single item that contained two tickets to the local ballet, dinner for two at a restaurant near the theater and limousine service. When deciding on what to combine, be careful that the items are a natural fit because if they aren't, they will be less likely to sell. You wouldn't pair five visits to a local yoga studio with a gift certificate for three days of doggy day care.

Mark down items toward the end of the auction.

If any of your items have not received bids as time is running out, you may want to mark down the opening bid price. If your organization has one event per year and the item doesn't sell, it will either have to be stored until the following year, or maybe even not get used (e.g., a ticket to an event the following month). If you have an event later in the year that the item could sell at or if it would be a good thank you gift for a committee member, etc., it may be better to leave the price alone. Be aware of the hazards of marking down. First, if your event gets known for markdowns, regular attendees may refrain from bidding at the start, expecting to get the item for less later in the event. In addition, a "fire sale" could hurt the donor's feelings, especially if she is attending. It may be better to either return the item or save it for another event.

Offer a Buy It Now option.

Some auctions give guests the option of skipping the back-and-forth bidding and instead buying the item at a premium (or for more than retail value). *Buy It Now* items can sell for as little as 25 percent over value (so a $100 item would be $125) to 200 percent or more. For

> *Buy It Now*: the ability for guests to purchase an item, at a premium price, so they don't have to bid against other people.

some events, this can be a great revenue builder. When trying to decide where to set the price, if your event is not new, look at what items typically sell for. If they tend to go at retail or below, 25 percent is probably a good choice. If items often go for more than retail, higher may be better. You can also do this by category or by item, making the Buy It Now percentage more for some than others. If you do have Buy It Now, be sure it is clearly marked on the bid sheets so guests understand that it is a maximum price and guaranteed to be theirs if they pay the Buy It Now price. Volunteers should also keep a look out for those items sold via Buy It Now so they can either X out the remaining bidding area on the bid sheets to make sure no one else bids, or remove the items from the table. For items that are "priceless," such as the opportunity to have lunch with a TV celebrity, you may not want to offer this option.

Consider using a company that specializes in auction items.

As noted in the live auction section, you can use a company to provide items on consignment. Prior to your event, you receive the item, perhaps a guitar signed by Taylor Swift, and if you sell it, you pay the company a predetermined amount. Assuming the winning bid exceeds the price you paid, you keep the difference. The positives: Procuring items is easy, and you can often obtain items that are nearly impossible to get donated. The negatives: if you can't get the minimum bid, you make nothing and if you sell it, you're giving away dollars to the consignment company that could have been yours. If your auction committee is strong and is great at soliciting, you probably don't need such companies. If not, it can be a great way to boost revenue or add some panache to your auction with a handful of unusual or hard to get items.

You may want to use an auction software company.

There are numerous companies, many full-service, that provide auction software enabling guests to both look at and bid for silent auction items from a smartphone. Deciding whether or not to use a service often becomes a cost-benefit analysis to determine whether you can net more money with—or without—the service. Here are some of the pros and cons of using an outside company.

USING AN AUCTION SOFTWARE COMPANY	
PROS	• *Both shopping and bidding is easier.* Guests don't have to continually return to the auction tables to shop or bid for items they are interested in purchasing. Their smartphone holds all the data for bidding (and many even let you "watch" an item or plug in a top price). Search options also allow bidders to look for certain items, and guests who leave before the bidding closes can continue bidding. • *Closing the auction is easy.* Unlike a paper auction, auctions using technology close at a pre-set time. There is no need for volunteers to circle winning bids, pick up auction sheets or do anything else. The technology announces how much time is left a few minutes out and then closes the auction, blocking bidding. It's fast and easy, and no one can "sneak in" and bid after the auction is officially closed, which can happen with paper auctions. • *Post-event auction checkout and cleanup is often easier.* Winners are immediately notified at the close of the auction so need not return to the tables to find out. That makes it easier to get attendees to collect their items before leaving, minimizing the number of guests needing to pick up or have an item mailed or delivered. In addition, auction software often collects key data (phone number, payment information, etc.) making check-out faster, with the added perk of providing attendee information.

CONS	• *Signing up to use the auction software is not as easy for the guest.* Some guests won't want to go through the process (even though most companies have shortened it as much as possible) or just may not be technologically savvy enough. As these companies become more and more common at events, this has become less of an issue. • *Set-up time can be longer.* While the reporting functions are often amazing, getting the items into the software can often take more time than the bid sheet system. Most software allows an upload of a master spreadsheet, but adding pictures or items received after the major upload can be time-consuming. • *It can be expensive.* Companies can charge in a variety of ways: flat fee, flat fee plus a percentage of sales or just a percentage of sales. It is often expensive, especially if you have a lot of staff from the company at the event to help guests get registered, etc. For repeat events, look carefully at typical silent auction proceeds, what percentage of retail you typically make and what you brought in this year before making a final decision on whether to use an outside company. Events that are new or have smaller numbers of items may call for paper and pen until the auction is more established.

Silent Auction Logistics

Staffing your silent auction.

It takes quite a few volunteers or staff members to run a silent auction. If you use a technology company to run it, the fee usually includes some staff to help you, but you will still need volunteers.

STAFFING YOUR SILENT AUCTION			
Volunteer Job	**Number of Volunteers**	**Tasks**	**Approximate Hours**
Silent auction preparation	1 or 2 for auctions with fewer than 50 items; 3 to 5 for 50+ item auctions	Create displays, bid sheets or upload information to auction technology; pickup items	3 – 20+ hours, plus time to pickup items
Silent auction set-up	1 or 2 for auctions with fewer than 50 items; 3 to 5 for 50+ item auctions	Set up display tables	2 to 5 hours if displays are prepared ahead of time and just need to be arranged
Guest check-in	2 to 4, depending on number of guests and how they enter (Staggered entry reduces the number needed.)	Prepare guests for bidding (either via paper bidding or technology). If you aren't collecting bidder information at the beginning of the event, you won't need these volunteers.	An hour to 90 minutes; usually 15 minutes prior to start of event through one hour into event start time (One volunteer should always be at the table in case a guest wants to register later in the event or pay for a Buy It Now item.)

Volunteer Job	Number of Volunteers	Tasks	Approximate Hours
Monitors and closers	2 to 6 depending on physical size of the auction	Answer guests' questions, encourage bidding, watch over items to keep them secure; close auction (circle winning bid, etc.) if paper auction; group items for guests winning more than one to pick up after payment	From start of event through auction close and cleanup
Checkout table	3 to 6+, depending on number of items and guests; there can almost never be too many volunteers at checkout	Process payments, deliver items to guests, help manage lines for checkout, check receipts at exit to ensure items have been paid for, help guests bring large items to their cars	15 minutes before auction close until last guest gets his items
Cleanup	2 to 4, depending on number of items	Clean up auction tables, pack items that are unsold or not picked up	An hour or less; after last guests picks up their items until complete

Non-Software Silent Auction Tools

Silent auctions that are done with paper and pen, instead of with tablet or smartphone technology, are often handled in the following way:

Auction Master Spreadsheet

This consolidates all the information about your auction. Via mail merge, you can use this document to create the display document, bid sheet and thank you letters/acknowledgements for both donors and winning bidders. The auction master spreadsheet, most often created in Excel, usually contains the following:

MASTER SPREADSHEET COLUMNS	EXAMPLE
Item Name	Tory Burch Scarf
Item Description	Traveler scarf
Item Category	Fashion
Item Number	01
Retail Value	$250

MASTER SPREADSHEET COLUMNS	EXAMPLE
Opening Bid	$125
Bid Increments	$50
Special Instructions	—-
Buy It Now	$325
Donor	Tory Burch
Donor Address	123 Main Street
Contact	Lisa Smith
Contact Phone	123.456.7890
Contact email	lsmith@tory.com

These next columns would be completed after the event with the winning bidder information to be used for thank you/acknowledgement letters after the event.

MASTER SPREADSHEET COLUMNS	EXAMPLE
Winner Name	Jane Doe
Address	25 Spring St.
City	Any town
State	Any state
Zip	00000
Phone	987.654.3210
Email	jdoe@email.com
Winning Bid Amount	$300
Paid Y/N	Y
Payment Method	Amex

To get your FREE downloadable sample Auction Master Spreadsheet and Bid Sheet, visit docs.AtoZEventFundraising.com.

Note that a similar spreadsheet, provided by your vendor, will likely be needed if you are using auction software.

Bid Sheets

Guests use these to bid. These sheets should have a description of the item, any exceptions or expiration dates, the retail value, the bid increment amount, the starting bid and a place for the guest to write her name, contact information (usually phone and/or email) and bid amount. If you are offering a Buy It Now option, this should also be listed, ideally at the bottom, separate from the regular bidding. If a guest does Buy It Now during the event, the regular portion of the bid sheet should be X'd through by a volunteer so guests know that there is no bidding, or you can simply remove it from the table. There should be at least two copies of the bid sheet; some events use three. That way your guest has a receipt, and you have a copy. There is carbonless paper (one sheet white, one sheet yellow) that runs through regular printers for just this purpose. If you are using smartphone technology for bidding, you will not need bid sheets.

Thank you letter/acknowledgement for winners and donors

Both the winning bidder and the donor should receive thank you letters after the event, ideally within 30 days, the earlier the better. Include the purchase amount and the retail value, which may be needed for tax purposes.

Displays

Display items on tables (organized by categories, with easy to see signs labeling the categories). Experiences, or items such as gift cards, require a description since there is no item to display. You can put the description in a clear plexiglass frame, or something similar, so it is a bit easier to read, or you can include the information on a bid sheet.

Payment and Delivery of Items

Organizers should plan a payment method and, if at all possible, have the guests take the items after the event ends. If you are using auction software, credit card information is often collected when the guest registers for the auction. If you are using a paper system, you can still collect this information, but be sure you have security measures in place to protect your guests' credit card information.

Bidders who pre-register with their payment information can typically go through faster lines to get their items and leave more quickly after the auction. You do run the risk of inaccurate credit card information (especially if you are using the pen-and-paper method), so ALWAYS run credit cards immediately on expensive items or those that have a consignment value.

Though the goal is to have all sold items picked up at the event, it rarely happens. You will have to call any winners whose items remain and arrange pickup (ideally at a centrally located office) or delivery. For delivery, you can call a courier, with either your organization or the winner covering the cost. If the winner is to pay, tell him how much it will cost. Typically, the organization pays the courier and then charges the bidder, just to make it easier for him. For bigger items, you may want to increase the minimum bid to cover your delivery cost.

Real World Example:

A large painting valued at $1,000 is offered at a silent auction. Since it is difficult to transport, the item included delivery within a 15-mile radius of the event. The starting bid was set at $550 (50 percent of the value plus the $50 delivery fee).

It is not uncommon for a small percentage of sold, but not picked up, items to be abandoned after the auction, even after you call and leave several messages. If this happens, call the next bidder and offer to sell her the item at her highest bid. It's important to call back winners with unpicked-up items (especially if you don't have payment) as soon after the event as possible. Do this the next day, or at the latest the day after. (Yes, you read it right: the next day despite the fact that you are exhausted!)

Silent auctions can be great revenue-builders. Most of the time, it's better to start small. Focus on soliciting the best-quality items possible and getting the bidders in the room. From there, you can build your auction up bigger and better for future events.

Online Auctions

In an online auction everything takes places via the Web. List each item along with a photo, retail value, starting bid and bid increments on a website. There are many companies that can help you conduct such an auction.

Online auctions usually feature the same type of items as live and silent auctions. A key to success is the size and level of activity of your email list. The more items you have, the larger the list should be. An active social media following can also be very helpful in promoting your auction and active bidding.

Here are two situations that might make an online auction the best option:

- You have a national or international organization with widely dispersed members. As a result, it is difficult to assemble enough of them in person.

- Large one-day or multi-day events, such as festivals or "Taste of X City" events, also complicate efforts to gather bidders. With an online auction, attendees can learn about the items for sale, ideally bid on computers that are set up (or via smartphones) and continue to bid throughout the event or even a set number of days afterwards. These work well when there are a lot of attendees, but they need to be well advertised and have good signs so that the attendees are aware of them and know how to bid.

Real World Example:

An international organization with numerous chapters has a yearly online auction. The auction consists solely of packages donated by the chapters, including trips, items and experiences. The bidding is open to all chapter members for approximately two weeks. All of the proceeds benefit the organization, and the funds raised help keep the chapters' dues affordable and to support the ongoing philanthropic efforts of the organization.

Some online auction services include marketing the auction to their own lists, increasing your reach. That can be a big plus, but be sure to do your homework; find out how many subscribers there are, the average open rate, the percentage of retail their auctions bring in, the number of sold versus unsold items, etc. If your event has most of the components you need for a successful live or silent auction, you likely don't need an online auction as well.

How Do You Choose Which Auctions to Have, if Any?

Auctions are a great way to raise extra funds, but they often take a lot of work to be successful. Deciding whether to have an auction, as well as what type, depends on numerous factors. One important factor is how much help you have. A first-time event put on by a small staff may not be the best candidate for an extensive silent auction. Perhaps it's better not to have one the first year, or focus your energy on creating a small auction with 20 to 30 high-quality items. Or, put your efforts into three or four great live auction items and forgo the silent auction altogether.

Another important factor is your venue, including its cost. If your venue is small or there isn't a high-traffic area to put your auction, it may be best to invest your efforts in sponsorship and ticket sales instead. Or, if your space lacks a sound system or is very expensive, a live auction may not be the best route. Consider incremental costs associated with your auction. If you have to pay the venue more because you need another room, tent or you have to rent tables, linens or other décor, measure those expenses against what you can potentially earn in the auction. Your goal is always to net additional funds, so if you are unsure your auction will cover your costs, it may be best to forego it.

CHAPTER TO-DO LIST

✔ **Determine which type of auction(s), if any, to have.**

✔ **Create an auction committee, a solicitation list and letters.**

✔ **Hire an auction software company and/or auctioneer, if needed.**

✔ **Solicit items for auction.**

✔ **Set up systems and create auction paperwork and displays.**

✔ **Recruit auction volunteers.**

OTHER REVENUE SOURCES

In This Chapter

✔ Paddle raises (also known as "fund a need")

✔ Raffles

✔ Peer-to-peer fundraising

Although sponsorships, ticket sales and auctions are the most common sources of revenue at an event, there are a few other ways to raise additional money. This chapter will explore a few of the most popular.

Paddle Raises

Events often include a **paddle raise,** a live solicitation for donations, which can be a great way to increase revenue and work best when you have either a live auction or a stage presentation. A few ways to make a paddle raise most successful include:

paddle raise: a solicitation of donations, typically via an auctioneer or event emcee, from event guests; also called, paddle call, fund a need or special appeal

Hold the paddle raise as close to the impact portion of your event as possible.

The best time to do this is just after you have told your audience about your cause and the impact you are making. Evoking emotion and showing your impact is extremely helpful when it comes to soliciting donations, similar to live auction bids. People are more likely to donate after they see how their funds can really help someone or something. (See Chapter 11.)

Offer a range of amounts, starting with the highest.

The auctioneer should ask guests to make a donation to the cause beginning with the highest amount first. Depending on the size of your event, this could be $5,000, $10,000 or more – or, it could be much less. From there, the auctioneer would continue to ask the guests to donate, with the amount decreasing. For example, a larger event paddle raise may ask for $25,000, $15,000, $10,000, $5,000, $2,500, $1,000, $500 and $250. A smaller event may start with $1,000, then move on to $750, $500, $250, $100, $50 and maybe even $25. Some events will create paddles with the different dollar amounts to be placed on the table. You can also use the paddles from your live auction. If the paddles are numbered (and linked to a guest), it can make it easier to record the donations, especially toward the end, when there may be a lot.

Tie your donation amounts to equivalencies or a specific goal.

Each paddle raise value should tie directly to the impact. For example, would $10,000 purchase a refrigerated truck to deliver fresh food to hungry people? Would $50 provide a week of diapers to a homeless child? Be sure you have variety rather than multiplied versions of the same one – so not $100 provides an hour of cancer research and $200 provides two hours. (See Chapter 11.) You can also tie the paddle raise to a specific goal. For example, if you want to raise $20,000 for a new piece of equipment, you could show a thermometer with your $20,000 goal. As you raise funds through the paddle raise, you can show the thermometer filling up. No matter which way you choose, let your audience know your goals or equivalencies by making sure your auctioneer has this important information and, if possible, include it in an A/V presentation. (See Chapter 11.)

Run your paddle raise with a lot of staff or volunteers.

At the outset only a handful of people will be donating, so it will easy to keep track of donors and payments. Once you get to smaller contributions (which will typically mean more donors), it can be mayhem capturing every donor's information and payment. It's an all-hands-on-deck moment, and it helps to have numerous staff members or volunteers spotting the donors and collecting the information.

Seed your audience with bidders, if possible.

If you have a donor who has committed to a gift prior to your event, ask her to make the donation public by raising her hand at your paddle raise. Jump-starting the giving, especially at the higher values, is a great way to generate momentum. Use real bidders, though, because it is unethical to seed the event with guests who aren't really donating.

TIP

Should donors receive gift for donating?

Maybe. A gift is an easy, visual way to recognize a donor. The most appropriate gifts are representative of your organization (e.g., a sapling for an environmental organization) or are related to the type of event (e.g., a cookbook at a food and beverage event). But it needs to make financial sense. The cost of such gifts must not exceed donations, and although a nice touch, it's not necessary.

Real World Example:

A seated dinner event held a paddle raise at the end of the live auction with donations starting at $5,000 and stepping down to $100. Since the décor had a butterfly theme, each guest who made a donation received a different-size silk butterfly with the larger donors receiving the biggest ones. At one table, each guest committed to giving at least $100 and then fashioned his or her butterfly into a piece of jewelry (necklace, bracelet, jacket lapel pin). It made a great photograph, and the organizers felt that receiving the butterfly pushed each table member to contribute at least the minimum, for a table total of $1,500.

Raffles

A raffle can be another great money-maker. There are many types.

Type of raffle	How it works	When it works best
Traditional raffle	Typically, there are one to three larger prizes. Tickets are sold throughout the event (and maybe even prior to the event), and winner(s) are drawn toward the end. Usually both the prize and ticket price are on the bigger side (e.g., a car, trip, cash prize with tickets selling for $100-$250 or more).	More expensive ticket events such as galas, food and beverage events, multi-day festivals
"Jar" raffle	There are multiple prizes offered and a ticket jar in front of each item. Guests buy tickets and put them into whichever prize they want to win. Toward the end of the event, a winner for each prize is chosen from its jar.	Event with a less expensive ticket, when you don't have enough items for a silent auction, family-friendly events
50/50 raffle	Tickets are sold throughout the event. At the end of the event, one ticket is drawn and 50% of the money collected is awarded to the winner. The other 50% goes to the organization. To be most successful, have several people walking around selling tickets.	This can be done at almost any type of event. It is great to periodically announce the amount collected to get more people to buy tickets.
Item pull	There is a set number of items (for example, wine, costume jewelry, etc.). Most are inexpensive, but there are a handful of more expensive items and at least one very expensive items. Guests purchase tickets and can "pull" an item, taking the chance that they will get one of the more expensive ones. You can use different methods to ensure that no one can see the items (e.g., by numbering them). *If you decide to do wine, be sure to check local rules for raffling alcohol.	Food and beverage events are a good match for this type of raffle.
Reverse raffle	Tickets are sold for a cash prize. Toward the end of the event, numbers are picked until only ten remain. Those ten guests can either split the prize amongst themselves or try to pick their own ticket in hopes of winning the grand prize on their own. If the person does not pick the winning ticket, the process starts over with the nine remaining ticket holders and continues until there is a winner or everyone left agrees to share the prize.	Event with seating, such as a dinner

When hosting a raffle, here are a few things to consider:

The prize(s)

Raffle prizes can vary a lot. Some raffles go big and have one large grand prize – a trip, a car, a large cash prize. On the other end of the spectrum, you may have multiple smaller items. When choosing the ticket price and how many to sell, consider the prize's value. A good rule of thumb is to limit the cost of the prize to 50 percent of your total sales goal. If you are doing multiple raffles, you may want to consider different prizes, sell the tickets for different amounts or set a maximum number of tickets to sell. If you can get a prize donated, even better as 100 percent of sales will go to your nonprofit.

Selling the tickets

This is a key factor in the success of your raffle. While you can sell tickets at the entrance, you'll do even better if your volunteers walk around to sell. When soliciting volunteers to sell tickets, you want to be sure you have someone who is comfortable talking to people he doesn't know, but also good at sales in general. It takes a special person to assess a crowd, break into conversations and begin a mini sales pitch. You also need to make the purchase easy; many guests won't have cash or a check, so make sure you have a way to charge a bidder or take a credit card.

Check the laws.

Raffles fall into a different category of income, so be sure you check to see what your local regulations are and if there are any fees or reporting required. A quick Internet search on "raffle law" along with your city or county is a good way to start. Large prizes may have tax implications for you and the winner as well, so be sure you do your research.

Peer-to-Peer Fundraising

In **peer-to-peer fundraising,** participants at your event ask their friends to make a donation to your organization on their behalf. Commonly used for athletic events, this method not only brings in additional money; it also can expand your reach to potential new supporters.

Peer-to-peer fundraising: soliciting donations by asking participants to reach out to friends, coworkers and family members to make donations on their behalf; also called team fundraising or social fundraising

There are different methods for encouraging participants to solicit the donations. For an athletic event, some organizations will waive an entry fee but require a minimum amount of fundraising. This is very common at larger events, such as the New York or Boston Marathon, where obtaining a runner number can be challenging otherwise. Numerous large organizations give numbers, and often training, to participants who commit to raising a certain amount of money. Some events will use a combination of methods; there could be an entry fee *and* a request (but not a requirement) that participants fundraise.

Should you give a prize or gift to your donors that reach certain fundraising levels? Again, this question has no sure answer. Sometimes a small gift, such as a T-shirt, can be motivating for people and produce better results. But, be cautious that you aren't spending a lot to make a little. For first-time events, it is prudent to skip a gift (unless it's at a very high fundraising level), or minimally, purchase something that is either not too expensive or doesn't require a large minimum purchase.

There are many companies that provide the tools (usually, but not always, online) to encourage and simplify peer-to-peer fundraising. They can be expensive, so they are probably best for larger organizations or well-established events with supporters who are strongly committed to your organization and its mission.

Chapter To-Do List

✔ **Determine if you will use any of the fundraising methods in this chapter.**

✔ **For a paddle raise, decide on donation levels and match equivalencies to each level.**

✔ **For raffles, choose which method you would like to use, check raffle rules in your area and solicit prize(s).**

✔ **For-peer-to peer fundraising, set up processes for participants to solicit donations or choose a program to help you.**

7

IN-KIND DONATIONS AND HOW TO CONTROL EXPENSES

In This Chapter

- ✔ **In-kind donations**

- ✔ **In-kind sponsorships**

- ✔ **How to control expenses**

In-kind Donations

Selling sponsorships, auction items and tickets is one way to produce a higher net, and saving money through **in-kind** donations is another. An in-kind donation is a good or service that a business provides you at no cost or at a discount. Such donations can cut your costs significantly.

in-kind: a donation of goods or services

You can solicit in-kind donations for almost anything that you would need to purchase or want to auction, but here are a few of the most common.

Venue rental

Some venue owners will donate all or part of the rental fee for nonprofit organizations. If a full donation isn't possible, ask if there is a nonprofit rate, as
there often is.

Food and beverage

This can be one of your largest expenses. Here are ideas on how to get some
of your food and beverage donated.

Type of event	Food and beverage needs	In-kind potential
Athletic event	Post-race snacks, water along course and post-race	• Local grocery stores may donate post-race items, such as bananas or water. Some will also allow organizations to pick up baked goods at closing the night prior to the expiration date, if pre-arranged. • Local bakeries or bagel shops for baked goods or bagels • Warehouse stores (e.g., Costco, Sam's) for bagels, granola bars, bananas or cases of water. Typically, there are online applications for these donations, and they need to be done a minimum of 30 days in advance. If you can't get a donation, purchasing items needed at warehouse stores also saves. • Local restaurants
Food and beverage events	Food	• Ask local restaurants to provide a booth/table at a tasting event. You can ask this to be 100%-donated, or use a system that reimburses them (all or partially) for the items purchased by attendees. For example, attendees buy tickets for $2 each with food ranging in cost from 1-4 tickets. For each ticket the restaurant redeems, they receive $1 to cover their costs, and potentially make a profit. • At seated dinners, ask caterers if they will provide the food at cost, cost plus labor, or a discount. • Ask wholesale food suppliers to donate a menu item. This works especially well for proteins. For example, a local food supplier donates 600 chicken breasts to your hotel or caterer for a seated dinner, allowing the hotel or caterer to lower the entrée price.

Type of event	Food and beverage needs	In-kind potential
Food and beverage events (cont.)	Beverages (alcoholic)	• Ask a local distributor to donate the wine, beer and/or bottles of hard liquor for your bar. Also ask for items for your auction, after ensuring you've met any legal requirements in your city. Note: Getting a permit to receive donated alcohol can be time-consuming. Start early – several months in advance is recommended. • Pay a corkage fee, a charge paid to a venue or caterer for opening and serving wine that you provide, to your venue or caterer. Then purchase the consumption wines at a warehouse store, or ask a local distributor or package store to donate them. • Partner with a local brewery to donate beer for guests.
One-day/night events	Intermission drinks and snacks	See athletic event above.
Family-friendly events		• See athletic event above. • Food trucks are great for family-friendly events, but be sure to find out if there are minimum-purchase requirements.

Real World Example:

At the party after a 10K and half-marathon, as part of their sponsorship, a local high-end burger restaurant set up a grill and gave mini-hamburgers to all runners. The party increased the number of registrations significantly, and the restaurant showed locals how great its burgers tasted. An added perk: All racers got a "Buy one, get one" coupon in their goody bag, encouraging them to visit the restaurant after the event.

Event staff (e.g., servers, valets, bartenders)

Labor is always a bit tougher to get donated, but in some cases you may be able to get a discount. Another option is to recruit students from a local culinary school to volunteer.

A/V (lighting, staging, sound)

A lot of A/V costs involve labor, but some companies will donate all or part of the "rental" costs for items like screens, large-screen televisions and stages.

Rentals

Some companies may donate 100 percent of the rental costs of items such as tables, chairs, service ware, glassware, linens and table decorations. Others may offer a discount or waive the rental fees if you pay labor (delivery, set up, pick up). Every little bit helps, so ask!

Entertainment (band, DJ, musicians) or auctioneer

Some auctioneers or entertainers may donate or discount their rates for non-profits. If you use the same entertainer or auctioneer for several events in one year, consider asking for a discount if you commit to all the events up front.

Printing

There can be quite a bit of printing for an event. You may need save-the-date cards and envelopes, invitations, RSVP cards, programs, signs, tickets and more. Discounts or donated printing can save a lot of money. If you are unable to get donations or discounts, ask two to four printers to provide quotes for all pieces you need printed. Some printers have in-house equipment, allowing them to give better prices on certain items. When that happens, it may be worth sending one job to one printer and giving another printer the rest of the job to keep prices lower.

"Ganging" your print jobs, or running several pieces as part of one big job, can save a huge amount of money. Anything that can be printed on the same type of paper should be done at the same time, if possible. One print job may include the save-the-date card, invitation, marketing cards, tickets and the cover of your program. A second print job closer to the event could be the program insides, printed on thinner paper, potentially in just black and white.

Advertising

Local media (magazines, newspapers, Internet) often want to be a part of events in their city. Many will give away a limited amount of advertising per issue to help nonprofits, often in exchange for a sponsorship. (See Chapter 10.)

Gift bags

You may want to have a gift bag for honorees, VIP guests or all guests at an event. Many businesses are willing to donate items both to help out a non-profit and to advertise.

Public relations and graphic design.

Some public relations and design companies take on a set amount of pro bono projects per year to help non-profits. For some, it may be a win-win if their clients can participate in your event in some way. An example may be a public relations company that specializes in restaurants may be able to coordinate with you to have one of their chefs do a demonstration at your event.

How to Make the Most of In-kind Donations

Always ask your vendors if a donation is possible.

Take a look at your expense budget. Is there anything else you can get donated or at a discount? Even if your vendors are unable to give you a 100 percent discount, any amount will be money straight to your event's bottom line.

Offer in-kind donors benefits, if you can.

Showing appreciation with tickets, logos in advertisements, etc. can be a great way to thank your donors and make it more likely that they will help both this time and in the future. Again, you need to balance what you give versus what you receive. You don't want to give away $1,000 worth of tickets to an event that typically sells out to get $750 worth of flower arrangements. In that instance, you'd be better off paying for the florals, perhaps with a nonprofit discount.

Companies new to your area are often good prospects.

Making a donation in exchange for sponsorship can be a wonderful way for a new company to get its name out into the public. If the company is unable to donate completely, offer to pay labor (delivery, set up, etc.) or hard costs (e.g., the cost to dry clean linens you would receive from a linen company). This could be a great win-win for you and the new company.

In-kind Sponsorships

When you are asking a donor for a substantial donation, it is often helpful to make the donor an in-kind sponsor. In-kind sponsors may receive the same benefits that a cash sponsor does at the appropriate level. For example, if your Silver sponsorship level is $5,000 and your venue gives you a $5,000 discount, the venue becomes one of your Silver sponsors and receives the benefits listed on your sponsor deck. Giving donors sponsorship credit (or marketing reach) gives them a WIFM (what's in it for me) that often can be the tipping point in getting them to make the donation.

Another, more popular option, is to give donors sponsorship credit at a percentage of the retail value of their donation, or at one sponsor level below the cash value. For instance, the donor in the previous example may get the $3,500 Bronze sponsorship level (70% of the retail value of the $5,000 donation, or one level below Silver) because it isn't a cash sponsorship. Another option is to keep the benefits identical except the number of tickets they receive for non-cash sponsorships is less. Whatever you decide, try to be consistent so that one in-kind sponsor isn't getting significantly more than another. (People talk more than you think!) This is an especially good tactic for events that have limited capacities so you don't end up giving away too many of your tickets.

One exception to the "keep it fair" rule is for media sponsors. Media sponsorships often have their own category on the sponsor deck (listed as "Media Sponsor," versus Gold, Silver, etc.) and their own set of benefits. (See Chapter 10.) The sponsor benefits are usually less than the retail value of the advertising or promotion being donated. Be creative though; media often want the opportunity to spread the word about their publication or station. Benefits such as handing guests a copy of the magazine as they exit, placing the magazine in gift bags, displaying a sign with a photo of a station's news anchor or the cover of a magazine often appeal to potential media sponsors.

How to Control Expenses

Another way to save money is to not spend it. There are often ways to cut overhead or eliminate items that aren't needed. A few to consider are:

Venue

The time of year and day of the week you choose can significantly impact your venue cost. A golf tournament on a weekend is usually much more expensive than one on a weekday. Explore the differences in pricing based on day of the week and season and then think about your guests and when they will be more or less likely to attend.

Décor

While you want your event to be pleasing and its ambiance to match the ticket price, décor is an easy place to overspend. You may find it hard to resist attractive specialty linens, chair covers, furniture and plants, but weigh the costs and benefits carefully. Ask your vendor if there are less expensive, but similar, alternatives. When choosing your venue, be sure to ask what's included. If a slightly more expensive venue saves you money because you don't need to purchase linens or rent chairs, it may be the better choice.

Real World Example:

At a seated dinner, the venue provided plain white linens for the tables. The event had a high ticket price, so organizers wanted the room to also look high end. They considered renting specialty linens for every table. Instead, they rented linens for every other table and, on the others, placed a coordinating long, narrow linen (one that is typically used to wrap a chair), as a table runner instead. The small change saved nearly $400.

Florals

Flower arrangements are beautiful, but they can also be costly. Carefully consider your floral needs and explore if there are other options that may work just as well. A handful of flower arrangements (e.g., at the check-in table or live auction table), in combination with other décor items such as candles in hurricane lamps, votive candles on mirrors or vases with fresh fruit, can also be beautiful. Live plants, perhaps orchids, are another alternative, and you can even sell them as part of the silent auction at a "buy it now" price that would help you recoup the cost.

Beverage

Beverages can be expensive. Some venues will permit nonprofits to purchase their own alcoholic beverages (typically wine) and will charge only a corkage fee (for opening and serving). This can be a big cost-saver, and don't be afraid to negotiate the corkage fee. Other ways to save money on beverage include: limit the offerings to wine, beer and non-alcoholic beverages only, offer only call brands (versus premium), close the bar during your program or immediately after the event (or make it a cash bar). Be sure to take your ticket price into consideration when making these decisions. A guest of a gala event with a $500 per person ticket will likely expect a full open bar; a $50 ticket likely won't.

Postage

If you are mailing invitations, their size and weight can significantly affect the postage. When considering a design, check with your post office to see what the cost would be before going to print. In addition, keep in mind that if you use the nonprofit rate or a bulk rate to send your invitations, delivery is unpredictable at best. First Class mailing, though more expensive, typically will be received in one to three days when mailed to your city or the surrounding area. Items sent at the nonprofit rate can take much longer and can arrive at wildly varying times. If your material is time-sensitive at all, go with First Class or perhaps pre-sort (if you have a minimum of 500 for First Class, 200 for standard mail). When in doubt, talk to your local post office or a company that specializes in mailing.

Real World Example:

For a gala event, a designer donating its services created a beautiful 5 x 5 square invitation with matching envelope. When the invitation was mailed, it cost 20 percent more because it was a non-traditional size and had to be hand-stamped. A slight change in the design would have saved several hundred dollars.

Printing and signs

Both of these can be expensive. Carefully analyze what you really need and consider ways to lower the cost. Does your entire program have to be full-color? Could the cover be color and the inside black and white? An 8.5 x 11 booklet folded in half and stapled costs less than a program with an unusual shape, coil binding or expensive paper. Could some of your signs, such as a 5K welcome banner or your silent auction category signs, be used year after year? Can you save and reuse the auction paddles?

CHAPTER TO-DO LIST

✔ Analyze your event budget and ask for in-kind donations.

✔ Identify expenses that, if donated, could create in-kind sponsors and decide which level and benefits the in-kind donor would receive.

✔ Look for and implement other ways to cut expenses.

Part Three

The Role of Event Fundraising Supporters

To get your FREE copy of the A-to-Z Guide to Event Fundraising appendix full of useful tools, checklists, sample document and worksheets, visit **docs.AtoZEventFundraising.com.**

CHAPTER

8

BOARD OF DIRECTORS

In This Chapter

✔ Board members as committee chairs or members

✔ Board members as volunteers

✔ Other ways board members can help

Boards of directors can help in numerous ways to make your event a success. Here are the most common ways:

Committee Members

Board members can chair or serve on one of your committees. Suggested committees include:

COMMITTEE	TASK
Auction	Help organize auction or solicit items
Sponsorship	Solicit sponsorships

COMMITTEE	TASK
Patron	Solicit patrons
Volunteers	Recruit, train and organize volunteers needed to run the event
Food & beverage	Manage food and beverage component of event. Depending on type of event, it could be choosing and managing a caterer, soliciting donations of snacks and water, or a variety of other needs
Ticket sales	Sell tickets, manage the ticket selling process and ticket selling incentives
Logistics	Help choose a venue, manage rentals, A/V, etc. For athletic events, manage security, road closures, permits, etc.
Marketing/public relations	Help with communications (e.g., website, e-blasts) and garnering awareness of the event through public relations (everything from writing a media alert or press release to negotiating media partnerships and recruiting local celebrities to emcee or participate) (See Chapter 10.)
Organizational impact/messaging	Help ensure attendees are educated about your organization, its mission and how spending money at the event can help your cause and community (See Chapter 11.)

Volunteers at the Event

If your board members don't want to commit to being part of the event committee, there is ample opportunity for them to volunteer at the event. You can use them as:

Greeters

It's great to have greeters to provide a friendly welcoming face. A "Welcome to XYZ Event and thanks for helping YY Organization" can go a long way in creating initial goodwill for your organization and can begin the sprinkling of your organizational impact message. Board members are great for this job because it is brief (usually 30 minutes or so while the majority of people arrive), allowing them to enjoy the event. Board members are also good choices to serve as VIP greeters for emcees, media, honored guests and top sponsors. Special guests often need someone to accompany them throughout the event to ensure that they are at the right place at the right time (e.g., if they are part of the stage presentation). Sometimes it is enough to simply provide a little special treatment at the beginning or inform the organization's executive director that the VIP has arrived.

Live auction or paddle-raise spotters or runners

Board members are a welcome addition to help spot bidders or to obtain bidder information so that they can pay for their items or make their donations. This may not be a good fit though if the board member is likely to bid or make a donation.

Auction checkout helpers

Another great short-term job for board members who are good under pressure is to help with auction checkout. No matter what you do to prepare, checkout is often mayhem. A few extra hands to direct lines, help run credit cards or help guests find their items or get them to their cars is always welcome.

Cleanup helpers

When an event is over, there is usually at least an hour of cleanup. Having a few people to assist both immediately after the event ends as well as a day or two later when you are reconciling auction items, etc. is always a benefit. Board members are great prospects for both tasks.

Other Ways Board Members Can Help

Selling tickets

Asking your board of directors to sell tickets is an excellent way to increase revenue and success. You can set a quota for the number of tickets each person is to sell, assign each board member a table (at seated events) to sell, have a contest, or simply encourage them to sell as many as possible. Any of these options should broaden your reach.

Real World Example:

In order to sell out an organization's golf tournament, each board member was asked to sell at least two foursomes. The outreach not only sold out the event, it brought in several new supporters.

Selling or providing leads for sponsorships

Even if your board member doesn't want to become an official part of your sponsorship committee, asking your board to help with sponsorship sales can increase your success. Some board members can be trained to ask for or help close sponsorships. Others can help by making a list or introducing the sponsorship committee to people or companies that may be willing to help the organization and its event. The longer your list of potential sponsors, the more you are likely to get, so engage as many people as possible to think of leads and help with solicitation and follow-up.

Recruiting committee members

Board members are often your most passionate cheerleaders. If you need committee members, ask your board to recruit family, friends or coworkers. Their passion will be contagious, and sharing it will often bring new people into important event planning roles.

Since all board members are not created equal and may already be committed to the organization in a multitude of ways, before asking them to help consider both their current workload for your organization and their particular skills. While it's good to make general requests to your entire board or other supporters, you often will be more successful if you make your requests specific and private. Be sensitive to what has already been asked of each person and try to match up the tasks you need the most help with to the person best able to provide it, without overburdening her.

CHAPTER TO-DO LIST

✓ Analyze your board members and decide who may be best at which tasks.

✓ Ask board members to commit to helping with these tasks; have a backup request ready in case he says no to your original ask.

✓ Provide information or resources needed for the board member to do the assigned task.

9

ROLE OF VOLUNTEERS

In This Chapter

✔ **Types of volunteers**

✔ **How to recruit volunteers**

✔ **Other "volunteer" roles**

✔ **Setting your volunteers up for success**

Event fundraisers are hard work, and the "it takes a village" anthem definitely applies. You will need many volunteers in numerous roles to make your event a success. You won't need all of these for every type of event, but this list should help you start planning.

Types of Volunteers

EVENT PLANNING VOLUNTEERS			
Volunteer Title	**Description**	**Events Where They Are Needed**	**Commitment Level**
Event chair(s)	The event chairman, or co-chairs, organizes the event with the help of committee members. They recruit committee chairs and members, work with the committee for event planning and implementation, as well as work with non-profit staff members on the overall event. Often, they run the committee meetings and help on committees or in areas that lack volunteers.	Most events, although sometimes a staff member from the organization fills this role	High
Committee chair(s)	Committee chairs head up the separate committees and ensure that the tasks are accomplished, with the help of the committee members.	Most events have a sponsorship, logistics, marketing/PR and ticket sales (could be participants) chair. Some events may have food & beverage, patron, auction and mission/impact.	High to medium depending on committee and how much is involved in each area (e.g., An event with a goal of 5 sponsors is much easier than one with 25.)
Committee members	Each of the committees listed above needs members to help. Depending on the committee, you may have 2 to as many as 10 or more additional people working with the chair(s) to accomplish the work.	Most events will have at least some committee members.	Medium

DAY-OF-EVENT VOLUNTEERS

Volunteer Title	Description	Events Where They Are Needed	Commitment Level
Setup	Volunteers to help set up the event	All	Low
Goody bag assemblers	If you have goody bags, you will need help assembling them and potentially handing them out at the event. Bags can be assembled prior to the event. You also need volunteers to solicit items to put in the bags.	Events with goody bags	Low
Greeters	Welcome attendees as they arrive. Potentially thank guests for attending at the end of the event and/or check auction receipts at the end to ensure that only items paid for leave with the guests.	Great for events such as galas, seated dinners, etc.	Low
Registration desk	Check in attendees. Could hand out numbers at an athletic event, work at will-call or media check-in, or handle other needs as guests arrive.	All	Low
Silent auction	Pre-event – Set up auction tables. During event - Sign up people for the auction, monitor and help guests bid, work at checkout table or help winners get their items. Immediately after the event - Clean and pack up the auction area. A day or two after the event - Help with follow-up (i.e. contacting winners of items not paid for or picked up, updating spreadsheets with final data, etc.)	Events with auctions	Low; medium if you require a training session prior to the event

Volunteer Title	Description	Events Where They Are Needed	Commitment Level
Live auction	Serve as spotters (people who watch the audience looking for bidders), obtain winner payments, deliver items to winners	Events with a live auction	Low; could also be volunteers serving other roles at the event
Photographer's assistant(s)	Work with photographer to point out people who need to be photographed and/or record names of people photographed. If you have a long event, splitting this into two shifts is helpful.	Any event with a photographer	Low
Stage manager or A/V helper	Ensure that things happen on stage or screen as planned (ensure people are near the stage on time, tell them when to enter and exit, help ensure the A/V manager queues up and shows the correct videos, PPT presentations, etc.)	An event with a complicated stage program or A/V program	Low
Golf or race course volunteers	People to be out on the race or golf course; includes ensuring safety (for example, pointing out a speed bump during a 5K), ensuring they are going the correct direction and cheering for participants.	Athletic events	Low
Food & beverage	Set up and man water tables for athletic events, pour water or wine at tasting events, etc.	Any events where food and beverage isn't 100% taken care of by the venue or caterer	Low
Cleanup	Don't underestimate the value of a dedicated cleanup crew. Committee members who have helped for hours prior to the event are often quick to leave once the event is over. If the number of tickets you have isn't limited (or nowhere near sellout close to the event), it can be worth giving free entry to a handful of people dedicated to cleanup.	All	Low

How to Recruit Volunteers

Volunteers are the key to an event running smoothly and not putting too much of a burden on the organizational staff. But how do you find volunteers? Here are a few ideas.

Committee Volunteers

Here are five ways to find volunteers for these higher-level-commitment positions:

Recruit within your own organization

If your organization has volunteers who come daily, weekly or even monthly, find out if they have shown an interest in being involved at a "higher" level or if their skills make them suitable for a committee that needs a chair or member. Advertise your needs in all the ways you typically communicate with volunteers (email blasts, website, newsletters, etc.). You never know who may be thinking about getting more involved or perhaps even needs some experience that could be turned into a resume-builder. In general, the best way to successfully fill most of your committee chairs and member positions is to just ask. A few people will step up on their own, but many more will become involved only if you ask them and tell them why you think they would be a good choice. If a person turns you down, think about other ways she could help, based on her reasons for saying no. For example, if she says she doesn't have enough time to chair the auction, maybe she could serve on the committee or help solicit items. Be prepared by having a list of open spots you need to fill and perhaps two or three other places a person may be able to help.

Real World Example:

One organization had a dedicated volunteer who helped each week with entering donations into the database and sending thank you letters. These data-entry skills were very similar to those needed for managing the silent auction items database that was part of the online tool the organization was using. The volunteer was delighted to help with this short-term project and freed up a significant amount of staff and auction committee time.

Recruit from last year's committee and volunteers.

If you have a repeat event, you may have had some day-of volunteers who really shined or said that they wanted to help more. Would any of them be a good fit for your open positions? This is also where succession planning comes in. In an ideal world, you'd have event (and committee) co-chairs, with one leading the event and the other supporting him and learning the ropes. The following year, the supporting one leads, and you bring in someone new to learn the ropes. This can happen with almost all the committees, but is especially important for the event chairman.

Ask committee members to invite new members.

Your committee members may have friends or coworkers who want to get more involved in a charity or may be great at some of the jobs you need done. Don't be afraid to have your committee help you recruit.

Recruit from your organization's own members.

If your organization has members, ask them to help! Many organizations require their members to volunteer a certain amount of time, and members can use the roles of committee chair or member to honor that commitment. Also, if the event is your organization's sole or main fundraiser, everyone should participate.

Ask local businesses.

Depending on the committee, you may be able to persuade a local business to donate its services and also provide committee members, maybe even a chair. A good committee for this is marketing/public relations. There are often local businesses that take on a handful of nonprofit clients to help their community. (See Chapter 10.) Committees handling design/graphics and food and beverage also have good potential.

Often it is difficult to fill all the open positions. Certain committee chairperson roles (e.g., sponsorship) are a harder sell than others. The goal is to fill as many as you can with helpful, competent people. You may need to tap your organization's staff to fill open roles, or try to get help from the committee chair(s) or board members.

Day-of-Event Volunteers

Day-of-event volunteers are a little easier to find. Sources of volunteers for low–level-commitment positions include:

Your own organization

Volunteers who help your organization on a weekly, monthly or even quarterly basis can be great day-of volunteers. If your organization has members (e.g., civic organizations like the Rotary or Kiwanis), your own members will make great volunteers. To keep track of who is doing what, you can simply post a sign-up sheet in the organization's common area or use an online (often free) website (e.g., SignUpGenius or VolunteerSpot). If you are using an online signup, be sure to advertise your need for volunteers via any communications you have such as e-blasts, newsletters or your website, with a link to the signup page.

Online

Many organizations have success using websites created to match volunteers with opportunities. Some examples are VolunteerMatch.org, VolunteerNow (volnow.org) and Idealist.org.

Your organization's partners

Does your organization raise money that they later grant to other nonprofits? For example, a Rotary Club hosts a 5K race with proceeds granted later in the year to other local non-profits. If so, ask your beneficiaries if they would help supply volunteers for your event. Lending a hand is a win-win for them as they will eventually receive funds for their organization from the event.

If a volunteer is new to your organization, be sensible when assigning her. It is always best to get to know a new volunteer before placing her in mission-critical roles, such as cash management, or high-pressure roles such as live auction payment collection or silent auction checkout.

Other "Volunteer" Roles

In addition to committee chairs, committee members and event-day volunteers, there are a few additional roles, that, while not what you think of traditionally as volunteer, can be helpful for your event.

Honorary Chairperson(s)

Some events benefit from the addition of an honorary chairperson. Typically, someone easily recognized in the community, this person helps raise the level of the event in the public's eyes. It could be a national or local celebrity, a media person, someone you would like to honor for doing a lot for your organization, or someone esteemed in the community you are reaching (e.g., a pediatrician who specializes in children's cancers for an event that raises money for children's cancer research).

When requesting someone to serve as honorary chair, try to keep your request modest, making it more likely she will say yes. Common requests include:

- Can we use your name and likeness in event promotion and post-event coverage?

- Will you attend the event? [You can mutually determine the time frame. Often influencers are unable to attend the entire event, so have your event flow in mind when discussing. Also, if the person can attend at only one specific time (e.g., the beginning), is your event flow flexible enough to accommodate that?]

- Are you willing to be photographed at the event?

- Are you willing to wear the event T-shirt and participate (e.g., lead the walk)?

- Can you mention the event—before, during or afterwards—in your company's communications, social media channels or media outlets? [If so, be sure to provide suggested messaging and hash tags, perhaps drafting posts that the honorary chairperson can customize. This makes it much easier for her to help you, while enabling you to manage the messaging better.]

Some organizations ask for a contribution to the charity, which could be a monetary donation or donation of an item you could sell at an auction. You could also ask the person to speak at the event: something as long as a keynote speech or as short as an announcement thanking people for coming and supporting the organization. In exchange, the organization usually provides complimentary tickets for the honorary chair and a guest (perhaps more so he can bring friends). Offering to pay travel expenses (could be airline and hotel for out-of-town guests, car service for local events) can also help.

If you are paying travel expenses, you need to tell the prospective honorary chair exactly what you are offering. If you have a set budget, let them know how much it is. If you are buying airfare, is it first-class or coach? Is your hotel 5-star? If the person commits, let her know if you will be making reservations and paying the expenses directly, or if she should do the booking and send you receipts for reimbursement. There are pros and cons for each option. If she pays, she may absorb the

TIP

cost (basically as a donation to the organization), which reduces your costs. If you reimburse her, you cannot control the costs or arrange for a hotel to donate a room or car rental company a vehicle.

Real World Example:

An honorary chair from out of state was invited to an event with a promise to pay travel expenses. After the event, the chair sent a receipt for reimbursement for two first-class airline tickets for a short 90-minute flight – one for him and one for his wife. The tickets were nearly 400% more than budgeted. Lesson: Be sure to tell the chair what you will pay for so there are no surprises! It's unusual for this to happen, but it does occasionally.

It is also common to give the chair a small thank-you gift. It can be presented on stage at the event or privately. The gift should not be too expensive as supporters don't want to see their donations go toward extravagant gifts.

One thing to keep in mind when engaging celebrities is that they often require some hand-holding and they can be demanding. Most often, it is worth the extra effort, but don't be surprised if your celebrity makes more than the average number of requests.

Host Committee

A host committee is another way to add prestige to your event, especially if it's a gala or seated dinner. Host committees are typically made up of people well known in your community who agree to both attend the event and to let you use their name in event marketing. Host committees can help distinguish your event from others, and often boost attendance because other community leaders may be more likely to attend when they see the host committee list. Complimentary tickets can be offered to these individuals, although the really dedicated ones often will pay because they understand that ticket revenue is part of the fundraiser. If possible, recognize these people at the event. You can list them on the event program, signs or the A/V presentation. Or give them a pin, special seating or a gift bag. An additional benefit of host committees is that often people who are dedicated enough to serve on one are also generous donors or auction bidders.

Emcee

An emcee from outside your organization can also be beneficial. A local celebrity or athlete is a great choice, as is a local media personality, especially one who will talk about your event on air. This works particularly well for drive-time radio hosts because they have large audiences and can "chat" a bit more than a TV host does. Emcees can be part of the ask of a media sponsorship, with a suggestion that he promote the event on air. (See Chapter 10.)

Setting up Your Volunteers for Success

Once you have put together a great roster of volunteers, it is your job to get them what they need to be most successful. Since volunteers will have only so much time to put into your event, provide everything you can so they can use the time in the most productive way. A few suggestions:

Job Descriptions

Volunteers need to know what is expected of them and what your organization will do to support them, especially if they are event or committee chairs. But even day-of volunteers can benefit from a job description that tells them their responsibilities, where and when they need to report, and who to go to with a problem or question. This document can include the dress code, where to store valuables, and where to park (and if there are parking fees or reimbursements). For committee chairs, provide this information either before or right after they commit to help. Day-of volunteers can receive this information a week or so in advance.

Past-event documents

Share any documents or information you have to help make things easier for the volunteer. You can provide the previous year's documents (or ones you used at a similar event) along with this year's information.

Training

Especially for the day of events, a training meeting will make the experience much better for both you and your volunteer. It can be a quick pre-event meeting with the basics or, for more complicated roles, a training a few days or even a week or two prior to the event.

✔ Determine volunteers needed for all phases of event (committees, day of, post-event).

✔ Create plan for recruiting volunteers.

✔ Recruit volunteers.

✔ Provide volunteers information, resources and training.

CHAPTER

10

MEDIA AND PUBLIC RELATIONS

chapter written by Allison Palestrini, Principal, Type A Development

In This Chapter

✔ What is an event public relations (PR) strategy?

✔ Identifying someone to guide your public relations

✔ Identifying media targets and lead times

✔ Crafting your PR pitch

✔ Creating your media and social media plan

✔ What to do before, during and after event for the most PR success

✔ Securing in-kind media sponsorships

✔ A PR strategy for when you are short on time or staff

Public Relations for Your Event

While we all think our event is the *most* special, the reality is that there are countless worthwhile causes and multiple fantastic nonprofit events in your city on any day of the year. (Our babies are also the cutest.) And while your PR efforts need to share the details of your event, the real opportunity for significant PR coverage (in front of another charity event) will likely come from telling the story of your organization's mission and what the funds raised from the event will accomplish. In this chapter, we will guide your PR so that all your time and effort generate success.

What is an Event Public Relations (PR) Strategy?

A PR strategy is more than a press release; it's a high-energy game plan to help educate your audience about both your event and your organization. What do you think of when you hear "Coca-Cola" or "Habitat for Humanity?" Surely your thoughts are influenced by your personal experience, advertising and marketing efforts, but a public relations strategy bridges the gaps with more frequent communications, effective messaging, influencer connections and media relations.

Public relations helps to tell your organization's story, so you don't rely on someone else to interpret your story. It gets your event and story on your audience's radar. Editorial coverage (also referred to as **earned media**) is trusted by consumers as more credible information than paid advertising. The metrics vary by expert and coverage type, as well as traditional media versus social media, but earned media coverage is typically 2.5 to 3 times more valuable than the paid advertising in the same publication or website (although it is difficult to measure because the weight and tone of the piece are factors in its value). No matter what the measurement is, it is valuable to have someone else talk about your event and organization.

> *earned media:* editorial coverage (versus advertising) in a printed publication such as a magazine or newspaper, broadcast (TV or radio) or online (digital newsletters, blogs, etc.)

Since you are not buying an advertisement, the media outlet has no obligation to run your entire press release or interview; rather, it will be the outlet's interpretation of that information. The reason you want to have PR support is to have that interpretation be the closest possible representation of your message, with the most possible coverage reaching your target audience. Which leads us to…

Identifying Someone to Guide Your Public Relations

Before drafting a PR strategy, it is important to consider your organization's bench strength and expertise in this area. Who will be leading the PR effort? Will that leader handle the strategy and big picture items, as well as the bulk of the tedious, but important work? Whether it's a staff member, volunteer, paid or in-kind PR professional leading your effort, that person will become a representative of your organization to the media, so *choose wisely*!

If a staff member isn't dedicated to communications support, there may be an opportunity to contract in-kind PR support from a professional PR practitioner or agency. (See Chapter 7.) Look for a local agency that works in your area of focus, or with similar constituents. For example, if your cause is a medical issue, is there a PR firm that has a dedicated healthcare PR team you could approach first?

A PR professional will have a leg up on anyone else you are considering. She understands the process and has media connections. Any time spent to secure a PR professional will pay off through time saved by not managing the effort in-house, and often will lead to better results.

Identifying Media Targets

If you don't hire a PR professional, you can still have great media results. The first step is to identify and understand the targets in your **media market**.

media market: region where the population receives the same or very similar magazines, TV stations, radio and newspapers

One way to determine your media market targets is to buy a list or purchase access to media databases. While these lists often provide a good insight to local media outlets, they often contain contacts that are either too broad or outdated. A "shot gun" approach of blasting your news to every single media contact you can find often fails; your communications are likely to go directly to a writer's junk or trash folder. For better results, use a shorter, more targeted list.

Building a thorough media list will likely take four to six hours PER market, depending on the media market's size. While time-consuming to build, a well-crafted media list is well worth the effort.

Get started early. The best approach is to thoroughly track the local media. Who is talking about similar topics? Who has a feel-good community column? After that, your next steps to building your media list are:

1. **Check MondoTimes.com for details on media outlets in your market(s).** This is your jumping-off point only. Some of these publications may no longer exist, and the list may not be comprehensive.

2. **Do an online search for newspapers, magazines, local TV stations and local radio stations in the market.** When you find an outlet, read through the website to determine who is the best contact. Try the "About Us" page, but you may also see bylines or other information that will give you a more direct route to a story. Look for calendar listings (both online and off), as well as editors and writers who focus on nonprofit organizations or charity events. Look also for columns or writers focusing on the type of work your organization does (e.g., a medical writer if your organization helps fight a disease).

3. **For events open to the public, search for online calendars that will post your details.** Yelp, Patch and Eventful are in most major markets and are great at reaching a larger audience. Most calendars list the who, what, when, where, and why and sometimes, even include a photo. Some calendar sites require a log-in process, which can make this time-consuming. Posting is NOT difficult. With confirmed copy and a photograph, this is something an intern could help with.

4. **Check editorial calendars of publications to see what their upcoming issues will feature.** Editorial calendars can often be found online as part of the advertising sales **media kit,** since publications sell advertisers on an issue being a good match for their product. If your event fits well into one of their upcoming editorial focuses, pitch your event and the story behind it specifically for that issue. Doing so will increase the potential for it to be covered; you may even get a larger story. Be aware of deadlines. Stories are often written three to four months before the publication hits newsstands, and plans about story content can be made even earlier. See below for more information about media **lead times.**

editorial calendars: a listing, typically by month or edition, about what the stories in the publication will be about; not every story will be part of the focus, but typically at least two or three will theme around the calendar

media kit: an advertising sales tool that contains information about the publication, including the number of people who are reached, advertising opportunities, pricing and often, an editorial calendar

lead time: the time between when a journalist receives a story assignment and when it is due

Engaging local influencers

Another benefit of your in-depth local market media reading is that you may start to identify local market influencers who could help with your event. Engaging these individuals and businesses adds excitement for participants and sponsors, and often sparks media interest in your event as well.

Who are these influencers? Perhaps a local celebrity or a radio or TV personality who would be willing to donate his or her time and help promote the event. Or possibly a government official (mayor, city council member) or a major business owner (ideally a sponsor) who is well known in the market. Once you've found and connected with local influencers, consider ways they can be involved with your event, such as emcee or honorary chairperson, and confirm their participation. (See Chapter 9.)

One important thing to consider if you select on-air talent from a TV or radio station to emcee your event or serve in another role: It may be difficult to secure coverage from another media outlet. For example, if you have signed up the NBC affiliate's news anchor, ABC's affiliate may not cover the event, (or at least not the part featuring its competitor). But it is unlikely that a TV station would refuse to cover your event because you have radio talent present or vice versa.

Media Lead Times

A basic understanding of lead times, or the time between when a writing assignment is given and then due, is critical. If you pitch your event after the deadline, not only will you miss the media coverage, you will also diminish your credibility as a PR representative. Lead times vary by outlet and by individual issue, so you should research each outlet's specific deadlines, but generally they are:

Type of Media	Lead Time	Additional Information
Online calendar event listings (such as an event guide by your local newspaper, online websites such as Yelp, etc.)	Most often, immediately to 48 hours from submitting to post time. Can be posted as soon as you have the basic event information, but be sure that your "call to action" (next steps you are asking the reader to take such as buy tickets, sign up online to volunteer, etc.) are ready to go. Most posts can be edited, so updates are possible.	Calendar event listings contain the who, what, when, where, why, and sometimes a photo. Listings often help increase an organization's search engine optimization (SEO), an indirect perk of taking the time to post.
Monthly magazines (print)	At least two months, ideally three months. For example, a March issue arrives mid-February, goes to press mid-January, so final editorial would likely be submitted in early January.	Since magazines have such a long lead time, post coverage will also run two to three months after your event as well.

Type of Media	Lead Time	Additional Information
Monthly magazines (online)	Two weeks to one month	Some magazines will have a blog, online photo galleries, social media, monthly e-blasts or dedicated event e-blasts
Weekly newspapers (print)	Two to three weeks out, perhaps a little longer	Publications like a weekly business chronicle or alternative weekly paper have larger pieces they work on for a few weeks. Regular columns usually have a shorter lead time.
Weekly newspapers (online)	One or two weeks	Event calendars, blogs, photo galleries and social media are possibilities.
Daily newspapers (print)	Week of event for daily sections and photos; one month for weekly sections	A weekly column might have more lead time than news coverage. Generally, the lead time is very short (both pre- and post-event).
Daily newspapers (online)	Week of event for daily sections and photos; two weeks to one month for weekly sections	Perhaps blog, photo gallery, social media
Radio	Short lead time: a few weeks to a month	Be sure to check to see if the local station has a syndicated show (played in multiple outside markets). If so, you'll need to tweak your pitch.
Local television	A few weeks for morning shows. For news coverage, send an alert a week in advance to get on the newsroom's radar, then again the day before OR the day of the event depending on the event time of day (not both).	Even if you are promised coverage, any breaking news can either delay or completely bump your coverage.

How to Craft Your PR Pitch

As soon as you start planning your event, you should begin thinking about what makes it newsworthy. Finding a way for your event to be newsworthy and being helpful to local media go a long way toward building a positive relationship and securing coverage. For your **PR pitch** to have the most success, you should:

> **PR pitch:** a story idea sent to a journalist

Be brief, get to the point, but don't be boring.

If your pitch is too complicated for you to explain briefly, how will readers ever understand? Remember that the subject matter is very familiar to you, but may be brand new to the recipient of your pitch. It is most effective to have standard press materials (a press release and/or fact sheet and local media alert) as a starting point, but gather everything you need to set yourself up for success. Know before you reach out if you have an interview subject, what you can share with media versus what you can't. Have photos.

Consider the WIFM (What's in it for me?) angle when working on your pitch.

Why would the media want to know about this? Because the paper has a community service column? Because you'll provide a photo opportunity with a local influencer at the event? Because it's your organization's 20th anniversary and you can tell what you have done for the community the last 20 years, and what you will achieve during the next 20? Does this event open the door to discuss the overall work of your organization? Include a personal note to the reporter and point out story angles with background in the press materials.

Review each media outlet online one last time.

Before you begin contacting media to pitch them, take a look at what they are covering and customize your pitch based on what you have been reading from the outlet and contact recently. If you are going to express an opinion about their coverage, it is most effective to express genuine opinions (not just rave about their last article, unless you really like it and can explain why it struck a chord).

Engage media effectively.

BE HELPFUL. Smart pitching to the right person at the right time is half of the PR media relations puzzle. Being EXTREMELY responsive to media inquiries is the other half. Be prepared to drop almost anything to respond to media.

Media are often on deadline, and finishing your story may be keeping your contact from going home at the end of the day. If a TV producer gets something else faster that will fit the bill, she probably will grab it. Don't waste the time you spent researching and pitching or miss out on coverage because you didn't get media what they needed quickly.

If you don't immediately have what's needed (e.g., if you are in the process of setting up an interview), let the person know you received the message and are working on it. If the reporter requested something more complicated (such as a specific photo or a quote from the event chairman that you are in the processing of obtaining), it is okay to ask about the deadline. Knowing when the story is due can help you gauge how much you have to rush.

More on pitching

You will feel like a broken record, repeating the same message time and time again. Here's an important thing to remember: While experts do not agree on the exact number of times a message must be received for it to be committed to memory (often 8 to 15), all agree that it is only through such repetition that you create an effective takeaway. What you are doing is consistently telling your story and spreading your message.

If you've done your research, but still aren't 100 percent sure of a reporter's current beat or area of focus – ask. Most will be helpful, but only if you've done as much homework as you can.

Avoid being overly familiar, unless you are friends in real life. Nicknames do not build instant relationships. If Jennifer Smith goes by Jenn, do not make the mistake of reaching out to her as Jen. Here's where being a bit more formal in addressing contacts will protect you.

Do not email ANY attachments.

Respect the writer's decision. Don't be a stalker – if it's not a fit, it's not a fit. The writer will let you know if he is interested.

Before you pitch, consider: Will you offer media complimentary (comp) access to attend the event? A discount for the journalist's guest? If the person is attending, make it easy for her: Provide parking information, where media check-in will be located, etc. Consider offering comps to potential media partners for the next year if you can fit it into your event budget.

While you would love every media outlet to cover your event, you will see, as you scan news coverage, that it isn't easy to figure out what makes the cut. Manage your expectations about whether your event will garner media coverage. Be creative and try to think about what would excite a reporter. Making your event stand out from others that are similar is a key to success and worth putting time into. But even with great pitch angles, you should be realistic about the extent of potential media coverage and share that information with your employer, board of directors, event committee, etc.

Media Outreach Plan

Once you've honed your pitch angles, you need to map out how you will use the media list you've created. This is when you need to consider timing. Compare the lead time of publications against your event timing and map out a calendar of who to pitch and when, along with any notes about pitch angles you think may have more success. Once you've completed that, prepare:

Press Materials

What best suits your event? A calendar listing? Media advisory? Full press release? If there are approval processes that must be met before sharing with the media, be sure to calculate that into your timeline.

Spokesperson

If you have a spokesperson, know when she is available and how to schedule interviews with her prior to speaking with media. If she is new to supporting your organization, you should provide talking points on the organization and the event. Depending on her background, you also may want to provide some media training.

Photo resources

Photos can help you obtain coverage and draw eyes to your event. To make it easy for the media, load photos to a file sharing site (e.g., Dropbox) and include detailed captions and photo credits, if needed. You can easily provide the link to the photo-sharing site, allowing the journalist to quickly see what you have and choose which photos are best for the story. The photos may include headshots of influencers who are connected to the event, your organization's logo, or people your organization helps.

Social Media Plan

Social media done well takes a lot of time and, like a media outreach plan, needs to be planned carefully. Which platforms do you want to be on? Facebook? Twitter? Instagram? Others? Once you understand one platform, another one suddenly becomes the rage. It is difficult to be everywhere. Consider your audience and your organizational and team strength to determine where you will focus your energy. Avoid the mistake of popping up with activity once a year around your event. That will not build loyalty and connection.

When you do decide which platform(s) you want to be on, consider the best way to do it well. If using Twitter, create a hashtag and promote its use before, during, and after the event. Can you tie Facebook into your photo booth? If you are using social media, do what you can to take advantage of your audience and influencers' followers.

One common mistake is handing social media responsibilities to an untrained young staff member or intern simply because he is comfortable with the platforms. Whoever manages your social media must be carefully trained on the messaging for both the event and your organization. Your social media manager will be the voice of your organization, so you must engage someone who will communicate in the appropriate tone and with the desired messages. If you don't have a staff member or volunteer who can do this, you can seek a professional to help via an in-kind donation or a discount.

It is also worth checking prices on social media ads. This is a constantly shifting landscape, but often for a small fee (and perhaps extremely small) you can **geo-target** by interest. This is a great option for large public events such as races and festivals because you can reach people who have similar interests in the geographic area close to your event.

geo-target: the ability to advertise to a specific geographic area, often by zip code, city or state.

To download sample press materials, visit
docs.AtoZEventFundraising.com.

Real World Example:

A civic group organizing a 5K ran Facebook ads that targeted runners and "friends" of the organization's page in the zip codes closest to the event. The group also ran "boosted posts," which placed the Facebook post higher on people's walls, making it more likely that they would see it. For only $30, the group expanded the advertising reach significantly and in a very focused way.

You Got the Story. Now What?

Your planning and pitching efforts have finally paid off. You've secured a story! Now be sure to:

Schedule media interviews and prepare the people who will be doing the interviews.

Provide briefing materials, as needed, to pre-identified participants such as the event spokesperson, local influencers, keynote speaker, award recipients or the event contact. Your briefing could contain:

- Event details pertinent to the interviewee, also known as a "run of show," which tells him the overall event flow and specifics about where to go and when. For example: "You will be interviewed by Jane Smith of XYZ newspaper at 7 p.m. You are to meet at the media check-in table, and then you will both be escorted to a *green room*, where you will be interviewed for 10-15 minutes."

> *green room:* a room used for special guests or for media interviews; it is typically seperate from the event space.

- Information about dress code

- Media updates, including coverage to date, expected media attendees, and anything else pertinent

- Message points (a refresher on the event, your organization, who it benefits)

- Specifics such as important notes for a live TV appearance on a morning show, or a pre-event phone interview. This is especially important if you've pitched a certain angle of the event to a reporter.

Determine process for capturing photos during the event and how you will get them after.

If you plan to do after-event PR, it is wise to hire a professional or skilled amateur photographer or, better yet, find one who will donate his services. Once you have one, send him a "shot list." This will detail all images you are hoping to capture, such as honorary chairs, special guests, and organizational leaders. If the photo is tied to an activity (e.g., the award presentation), include timing notes. These can be specific (8:05 p.m.) or related to your overall run of show (after live auction).

It is helpful to assign a volunteer (ideally someone who knows the people on the shot list if the photographer doesn't) to stay with the photographer to record the names of people in each photo.

To get your FREE downloadable sample press materials, visit docs.AtoZEventFundraising.com.

Once the event is over, how will you get photos from the photographer to local media who may be interested but were unable to attend? How quickly will you get them? Since time is often of the essence, it pays to plan ahead with your photographer and ensure that he sends you a handful of photos as early as the next day.

Lastly, if you are doing social media, be sure you have someone taking and posting pictures, as well as texting, during the event.

Media relations at the event

If you encourage media to attend your event, prepare a plan for greeting them. You may have a media check-in table near registration, or if it's just a few people, it may be a better use of staff time to have the reporter text a certain staffer or volunteer to greet him upon arrival. Whoever is serving as a contact for media at the event should be both briefed and provided the schedule or script for each media member.

After the Event

Post-event PR

Within a few days of the event, it is a good idea to send a follow-up press release that states the success of your event (often money raised) along with a few photos, sometimes including those with local influencers. This is especially helpful for local lifestyles magazines that profile events, along with attendees, in their "social" pages.

When reporting the amount raised, most nonprofits cite the gross amount (cash brought in via sponsorships, auctions, donations and ticket sales) rather than the net that the organization will receive, but either is acceptable.

If you can, get confirmation that a post-event story will run so you can be sure to get a copy. Thank the writer and share the coverage with your influencers, committee and organizational leaders.

Measure the results of PR efforts.

The volume and quality of **clips, media equivalencies** and website traffic are good to know, especially when comparing from year to year. You can use Google News alerts to monitor coverage. It's a good option and is free, but you may

clip: each instance that your event or organization gets mentioned in the media, for example, a story in a newspaper, an online blog post or a mention on TV or radio

media equivalencies: the benefit of PR efforts, typically measured as an equivalent to what the same space would cost if an advertisement were purchased; often a multiplier of 3 to 10 is applied for the additional credibility that news coverage gives, versus advertising

also find that its results aren't always comprehensive. There are clipping services that usually charge a monthly retainer, plus fees for each clip, to monitor coverage. This may or may not be worth the money, depending on the scope and team involved. Nor can you be sure that a service will catch everything that runs. Remember: Print coverage after your event may take a few months to appear in long-lead media such as magazines.

Measure the media impact of your event. Sharing coverage (major clips and number of people reached) with sponsors is a great addition to an event recap. In addition, showing that your event gets local coverage (including results such as XX number of people reached) can be a great sponsorship sales tool for the next year.

Maintain your relationships with influencers and media.

Thank the media, your emcees and any influencers who played a role in the event. You could simply email them, or you might send a handwritten note or even a small token gift (for an influencer with a larger role, such as emcee). These should be ongoing relationships!

Advertising through In-kind Sponsorship

Another form of in-kind sponsorship that may help promote your event, if it is open to the public, is advertising in one or more media outlets.

In-kind advertising sponsorships give you the opportunity to advertise your event to the sponsor's readers, which should boost attendance. More important, they can help you sell sponsorships. If your event typically attracts 750 people, that is one level of marketing outreach. If you run your sponsor's name or logo in an ad that reaches 10,000 readers, that is a much higher level. In addition, many media outlets will provide additional outreach opportunities such as event listings on their websites and emails to their databases. Securing an in-kind advertising sponsor is a good investment of time.

Who should pursue such a sponsorship? The PR committee or the sponsorship committee? While the PR team will most likely be the best choice to identify potential sponsors, it is often better to keep advertising outreach and editorial outreach separate. Once your PR chair has created a target list of media sponsors, have her work with your sponsorship chair to lead the outreach. This way the PR team can pitch all media freely (even the sponsor's competitors).

To determine the value of a sponsorship, research the outlet's advertising rates. Most media sales kits are available online and provide this information. If you want to propose donation of a half-page ad in a magazine, you should know what that would cost before you make your pitch. This will help you ask for an appropriate amount of coverage for the sponsorship level you are offering.

Who Do You Talk to and What Do You Ask for?

Select your media targets for potential partnership/in-kind support by evaluating the target audience for your event. Also evaluate what sort of support the outlet is providing to other organizations.

Type of Media	Who to Target	What to Ask for
Magazine	Publisher and/or executive editor, sometimes Marketing Director	Donated ad space in magazine, digital support (for example, e-newsletter, ad on website), reader give-away opportunity, ticket specials for readers, social media support
Newspaper	Marketing or community affairs department staff member	Same as magazine
TV station	Community affairs department staff member	Public service announcement (PSA) with a tag for your event (sometimes station will tape for you, sometimes you need to provide tape, known as B-Roll); on-air talent to serve as emcee or be featured at the event; digital support (e-newsletter, ad on website, calendar listing); social media support; opportunity to be a guest on lifestyle show to discuss event and organization
Radio	Marketing or community affairs department staff member	Commercials or PSA with tag for your event; digital items above
Billboard/outdoor advertising	Sales or marketing department staff member	Billboard space; traditional billboards have significant hard costs to print, so try companies with digital billboards first, if you can get the artwork created.

Do not limit yourself to traditional media outlets to connect with your target audience. Would a large banner displayed on a busy road help promote your event? Consider asking a business on that busy road to put such a banner up for you in exchange for an in-kind sponsorship. Be creative about ways to promote your event and how to connect with your target audience.

Some media want exclusive opportunities in either their category or across the board. Keep this in mind and approach your biggest, best target first. Ask for more benefits (e.g. two email blasts or a larger ad), if the outlet requires exclusivity.

What Do You Offer?

Why would a potential sponsor want to donate its product or services? Most often because of the exposure you can provide for the brand through your event's **activation** elements. Depending on the potential sponsor's marketing priorities, this may include logo inclusion in printed materials, a table at your event, tickets to your event, opportunities for its staff to volunteer at the event, distribution of printed materials in gift bags or at a table at the exit of your event, or branding for a portion of your event (e.g., cocktail hour sponsored by XYZ). You should aim to provide value to the sponsor that is in line with what you are requesting.

activation: the way that a sponsor's brand is showcased at an event or leading up to the event

When to Approach an Outlet Regarding In-kind Sponsorship

Like editorial deadlines, advertising deadlines are important. You can never approach a media outlet too early for a partnership. The contact may tell you to ask again at a future date, but that is far better than learning that you are too late. Check with potential media partners to find out if they choose nonprofit event partners on a rolling/year-round basis or have an annual planning session. If your target is unfamiliar with your organization or event and is not supporting it in the current year, you may want to offer complimentary tickets in hopes of partnering with the potential media sponsor the following year.

PR When Time or Staff is Short

The plan outlined above is ideal, but what if you have either limited time or staff to work on it? Below is a bare-bones list of what will likely deliver the best PR results in the least amount of time.

- Make a list of three to eight media outlets in your market that would create the most publicity to your target market. An online search for event-listing websites, community newspapers or magazines is a good place to start. For gala-type events, social magazines in your market are good prospects. Record a contact name and information.

- Create press materials needed to reach these outlets most effectively, such as a fact sheet, press release and media alert.

- Post online listings, pitch reporters (for editorial coverage) or appropriate contact (for in-kind media sponsorships). Respond as needed when you receive results.

- Write and post Facebook geo-targeted advertisements or boosted posts, especially for low-ticket-price events such as athletic events or one-day events.

- If during your research you found media outlets that publish stories after events, send a post-event release and photos, if you have them.

- Document your PR success for post-event sponsor recaps or for sponsorship proposals the following year.

CHAPTER TO-DO LIST

✔ **Determine who will manage your public relations.**

✔ **Create market list, determine media lead times and create pitching calendar.**

✔ **Work with sponsorship committee to secure in-kind media sponsorships, if possible.**

✔ **Create PR pitch and other resources needed to secure press; pitch the press.**

✔ **Implement your pre-, during- and post-event PR plan, including supplying those talking with the press with pertinent information about your event and organization.**

✔ **Document PR successes that you can use to thank influencers and sponsors and for sponsorship solicitations the following year.**

✔ **If time or staff is short, work through plan as outlined.**

Part Four

Creating Lasting Impact from Your Event Fundraiser

To get your FREE copy of the A-to-Z Guide to Event Fundraising appendix
full of useful tools, checklists, sample document and worksheets, visit
docs.AtoZEventFundraising.com.

CHAPTER

11

SHOWING ORGANIZATIONAL IMPACT AT YOUR EVENT

In This Chapter

✔ What to tell attendees about your organization

✔ Where to show organizational impact at your event

✔ Different opportunities to show organizational impact

While your event's main purpose is to raise money, it has the potential to help your organization in several other ways. If done correctly, your event can further educate and excite your sponsors and attendees, turning them into dedicated donors or supporters. The best way to do this is by showing your nonprofit's impact.

Organizational Impact

Most events attract a wide variety of people. Some may be long-time supporters such as volunteers, board members or repeat sponsors. Others may know very little about your organization. Showing **organizational impact**, or educating your attendees about your organization, is a great way to create new supporters— and to show current supporters that you are making progress toward your goals.

organizational impact: information about your organization, who it helps, how it differs from similar organizations and how it helps to improve the community or its issue

What to Tell Attendees

All events should have the following items to educate attendees about your organization and what it is accomplishing.

Logo

Be sure your organizational logo is front and center at the event.

Mission

Your guests should know your organization's mission by the time they leave. People are more likely to support an organization if they clearly understand what its mission is. Tell your guests multiple times in locations throughout the event, as well as before and after the event.

Statistics

Guests should have an understanding of the problem your organization is working to solve. A great way to do this is to share statistics about not only the problem you are working to solve, but also the progress you are making. For example, if your organization raises funds to end childhood cancer, you can tell you audience that "1 in 285 children will be diagnosed with cancer before the age of 20". If your organization works to improve high school graduation rates, share statistics such as "8 out of 10 of the teens that go through our program graduate from high school, compared to their peers where only 2 out of 10 graduate."

True stories

Never underestimate the power of a true **impact story** about what your organization has done to help someone or something. Testimonials of clients show your organization at work and should be shared with your attendees, donors, volunteers and other supporters. A current or past client revealing what life was like before being touched by your organization, and the improvement they have seen since, can be a very effective way of showing your organization's impact and why it is worth investing in it.

impact story: a story that demonstrate how your organization is making change in your community; they are personal stories, typically meant to evoke emotion, so that its audience wants to help your organization

Equivalencies

Equivalencies are a way of demonstrating how funds raised help your organization accomplish its goals. There are two types of equivalencies – macro-level and micro-level. Macro-level equivalencies provide statistics on your organization or the problem you are working to solve. For example:

equivalancies: a way of tying financial contributions to the mission of your organization; for example, $50 funds an hour of research to help end childhood cancer

- Every year XYZ Organization provides food and clothing to YY families.

- There are XX adults who suffer from YY in YOUR CITY or STATE.

- 3 in 10 families have XXX.

- With support from people like you, XXX Organization is able to do YYY.

These statistics help paint a picture of not only the problem your organization is working to solve, but also what it has accomplished toward that goal. Showing guests this information not only educates them about your organization, it reminds them why the event is taking place.

It is equally, if not more, important to have micro equivalencies, also called "dollar handles," which show what a specific dollar amount can achieve. Some examples:

- $10 provides diapers to a child in need for 3 days.

- $100 funds an hour of research to help find a cure for XX.

- $250 can plant a garden in a city that will provide fresh food for 30 families.

- $1,000 can provide XX medical services for YY patients.

- $5,000 can purchase XX equipment to help YY people with ZZ.

You should have dollar amounts ranging from low to high, with either what each of those amounts can buy (typically a repeat need) or items you plan to buy with the funds raised. Avoid taking the same equivalency and multiplying it to create a larger one (e.g. $25 buys school supplies for a child in need and $50 buys school supplies for two children in need.)

Where To Tell Attendees

You can tell your attendees about your organization's impact in a variety of ways. Here is a quick list of ways to keep your guests informed and engaged.

Signs and banners

Your logo, mission and both macro and micro equivalencies, as well as statistics about the problem your organization is working to solve, can be on signs spread throughout the event. Signs near the entrance (e.g., **a step and repeat wall** with your logo) and the exit (e.g., Thank you for attending and helping XX solve YY problem.) help ensure people know what organization they are supporting.

step and repeat wall: typically used for public relations, a banner with logos, or the same logo multiple times, large enough so that when photographs are taken in front of it, the logo is readable

At athletic events you can place signs near registration tables or hang banners on fences along or near the race course. If you have a stage, put signs on the corners of the stage, above the stage or even on the podium. Small table signs can also be used on flat surfaces such as dining tables and auction tables. Don't be afraid of being creative about how you show the information. Can it be worked into a floral arrangement? Is there something that represents what you do that can be used as a sign? If you have a photo booth, can a statistic be worked into the photos or the backdrop? If your organization is in human services, photographs of your clients (with their permission, of course) and some short explanatory text go a long way in telling your story and mission.

Real World Example:

At an event raising money for hungry children, instead of traditional table numbers, organizers printed the numbers on old-fashioned metal lunch boxes and added a statistic about hunger in the community. It was an innovative way to get guests to the right table while reminding them about the goal of the event—to end childhood hunger.

Printed materials

If your event has a program, ticket or any printed material that attendees receive (even the T-shirt or a goody bag for an athletic event), be sure you include information about your organization and how to make a donation. This is especially important for athletic events such as a 5K because attendees often don't have their wallets. If providing a donation envelope, make it easy for them to mail you the donation by putting the information on an envelope with your mailing address on it. Silent auction bid sheets (or as part of your electronic bidding system) are another great place to include your logo or an equivalency, such as "Your additional $25 bid will help XX people do YY."

A/V presentations

Are you planning to have A/V? If so, a video showing how your organization is doing its work is a great addition. Or, a speaker (e.g., past recipient of your services or person who has conquered what you are working to cure) can talk briefly about how your organization has helped her. Statistics worked into a rotating PowerPoint presentation or spoken by an announcer are also great ways to share information with attendees. (If you have a PowerPoint, remember to thank your sponsors.)

A giveaway at the event entrance

Do you want a physical sign of how many people have the problem you are trying to solve? Think about giving guests something when they enter that corresponds with your issue. For example, if 1 in 5 people have XX, give every 5th person a button or bracelet. At some point during the event, have recipients raise their hands. Not only is it a great way to show impact in an inexpensive way, it's also a great conversation-sparker!

Email blasts

Are you emailing information about your event? Be sure to include organizational impact in each communication. **Impact stories** work well in email blasts, in that they can be told via text and photos or a video. Thank you emails (for registration or ticket purchases) should also include your logo, mission and equivalencies.

Websites and social media

Incorporating organizational impact into the event page on your website, your registration page ("Your $30 registration can provide X to Y."), as well as in any social media, is a valuable addition to your awareness-and-impact plan.

Other

Providing your auctioneer with equivalencies can help jump bids to the next level. He might say, "Come on, folks! Another $500 can provide YY for XX." Micro equivalencies are especially helpful in a paddle raise (also known as fund the need) when you are asking for donations from the audience. (See Chapter 6.)

When in the Event You Should Tell Attendees

While it is important to remind attendees of your purpose in various ways throughout the event, it is especially important to remind them of impact and show equivalencies at key times, such as when guests are making donations or spending money. The only thing worse than not telling guests what their money can do, is telling them at the wrong time and missing the "moment."

If you have a video or speaker, the best time for your impact message is just before the live auction or paddle raise or right before the end of the silent auction. These fundraising moments should be halfway to two-thirds of the way into the event: not so early that they are just arriving and getting settled and not too close to the end, when some guests will begin to leave or lose interest.

While some may be reluctant to work the "heart strings" of your guests, evoking some emotion can help raise money. Be careful not to victimize anyone; focus on success stories and find people who believe your organization has helped them and who are willing to share their stories (either live or via a video). Live is often better, but be sure that your speaker has been coached so that he says your name and mission correctly and stays within your time limits. It's also important that the message is honest and within both of your comfort levels.

No matter how you choose to incorporate your organizational impact, make it part of your early planning. It not only will help your fundraising efforts, but will help move people into a deeper relationship with your organization. (See Chapter 12.)

CHAPTER TO-DO LIST

- ✔ Choose the method and location of conveying organizational impact to your guests.

- ✔ Create macro and micro organizational equivalencies, if you don't have them already.

- ✔ If your event includes a video or a speaker, make sure that the message is correct.

TURNING EVENT ATTENDEES INTO ORGANIZATION SUPPORTERS

In This Chapter

✔ How to capture attendee information

✔ How to turn attendees into supporters

✔ How to write a follow-up plan

It's easy to get so tied up in event planning that you miss an important opportunity to draw your event attendees further into your organization by converting them from attendees to supporters. Here are a few ways to help you accomplish this.

Capture Attendee Information

Turning attendees into supporters begins the moment you start planning the event. Capturing information about your attendees has to begin long before the doors to the event open to be most effective. So when can you do it?

At ticket purchase

One of the easiest places to capture information is when attendees buy tickets, especially if you are selling online. Credit card payments will likely provide basic information (name, address, email), but you also have the opportunity to capture other information. You may ask how the person heard about the event, demographic information (e.g., age, sex, and household income, which you can use for your sponsor deck). You might even ask a specific question that could help you win a potential sponsor. ("Do you plan to buy a car in the next year?") You can also ask if the ticket buyer would like more information about the organization or would be interested in volunteering, donating, etc.

You need to strike the proper balance between getting information about attendees and asking them so many questions that they abandon their purchase, so keep it short. Ticket purchase time is also a great opportunity to begin sharing information about your organization and the work you do, as well as some impact information. (See Chapter 11.)

Before the event

Some events feature a pre-party or patron party for high-level sponsors and special guests. Typically held anywhere from a month or so prior to the event, to as close as the day prior or even just before the event starts, this is an opportunity to thank important people in your event and provide organizational impact information. High-level sponsors, honorary chairs, host committee members, patrons and even key media may be on your invitation list. This party would be a fraction of the size of your actual event and can be as formal as an in-home catered party or much more casual.

Guests of this party may, or may not, attend your main event so it is important to capture contact information prior to the event (for example, through a RSVP process) or keep notes on who you speak to that is interested in becoming more involved and get their contact information, or minimally who invited them to attend so you can get it at a later date.

Why host an event like this? Often tickets to this party are one of the benefits to sponsors. For example, a gala event that comes with one table for ten, may offer just 2 or 4 tickets to the patron party. Although these parties often don't have a formal ask for donations, those done well have an impact portion of the event. This may be as informal as signs, or something more impactful such as a short speaking portion where a past recipient speaks about his positive relationship with your organization. If you are having a live or silent auction, providing a preview of the top items can also be beneficial.

If you do decide to host a pre-event, be sure to estimate the cost compared to benefit to ensure it is worthwhile.

At the entrance to the event

Another good place to capture information is at the entrance. Asking attendees to complete a brief entry form in hopes of winning a door prize is the most effective way to do this. Basic facts such as name, email and a phone number are a must. You can also include some of the information listed above, but brevity is better. If you are using paper tickets, you can print the door prize on the ticket (especially if you are asking more questions), allowing attendees to complete it before they arrive.

To get as many attendees as possible to compete for the door prize, be sure to have it located in a prominent area near the entrance. A high top table with a big fish bowl and a sign that says "Door Prize Drawing for XXXX" is very effective. In addition, be sure to have pens and extra door prize entry forms on the table (even if you have it printed on the ticket). Volunteers who are welcoming guests can ask them to complete the form by handing them one along with a pen. A stage announcement five minutes prior to the drawing alerting guests that they still have time to enter should reel in a few more entrants.

What about the prize? While the value of the prize can definitely influence the number of people who enter the drawing, even a small prize (tickets to next year's event?) is better than nothing. A trip for two to New York City will garner more entries, but it may be better to make it a live auction item. You need to choose wisely so you maximize revenue potential.

A sponsor that wants to gather attendee information is a good candidate to become the door prize sponsor. The sponsorship fees can be paid in cash (and you provide the prize), in-kind (donation of the prize itself) or ideally, a combination of in-kind and cash (e.g., a staycation getaway – one-night hotel stay and dinner for two donated by the sponsor plus $500 cash). If you do share the attendee information with the sponsor, let guests know on the door prize slip with a statement such as "Your private information will be used only by XYZ Organization along with XYZ Sponsor and will not be shared with any other parties."

During the event

Another sensible time to capture attendee information is during auctions and raffles. Whether you use an electronic system or paper bid sheets or entry forms, capturing name, phone number and email addresses can help build your database.

Turning Attendees into Supporters

Once you've gathered all your attendee information, add it to your database (or keep a spreadsheet) and tag the names with the event name so you know where they came from. You can invite them to future events, ask for year-end donations and more. In addition, depending on the guest's level of involvement in the event, you should also segment the list based on what other communications you have planned.

Email blast

For all attendees, an email blast thanking them for attending message is a smart first step. Ideally, it would go out within a few days after the event and contain not only a thank you, but also information about how much money was raised and the impact that money will have on your organization and its mission. For example, if your 5K race raised $3,000, tell people that and point out that the money is enough to provide 30 children an afterschool educational program.

Your email blast should contain a link to your website with information about how to learn more about your organization. It also could ask them to get more involved, perhaps as a volunteer, or to make a donation (but make it a very soft ask since they already have spent money with you). If you already know the date of next year's event, include a save-the-date message.

Acknowledgement letters/emails

Any auction purchasers should receive a letter thanking them for their purchase and providing the fair market value of the item and price they paid. Provide your organization's name and federal tax ID number. Most organizations include a statement that says the purchaser should contact her accountant to determine the tax-deductible amount, but in general, it is the amount paid in excess of the fair market value. So if you purchase a rug that has a value of $300 for $400, $100 would be deductible.

These letters should arrive soon after the event – ideally within a week or two, but no later than one month. Include information about the event such as amount raised and its impact, but also how to find out more your organization and any upcoming events.

Personal phone calls

Gulp! I know everyone just wants to send emails these days, but sometimes a phone call is in order. So when should you do this? When it makes sense as a stewardship activity. If someone makes a large donation during a paddle raise, purchases a live auction item or comes up to a staff member during an event to say he loves the organization (and maybe even expresses interest in doing more), call him. A few minutes on the phone with a genuine thank you can go a long way in strengthening the relationship and may move him to a higher level. While talking to the donor, try to find out why he made the donation or bought the item. What is his WIFM (what's in it for me)? Ask if he'd like to learn more about the organization. Perhaps he'd enjoy coming in for a tour, attending a volunteer or committee meeting or having coffee with a staff member. Even if you simply leave a voice mail, a personal thank you can go a long way.

Invite them to learn and do more.

Once you have these new attendees in your database, keep them informed. Whether it's via email, a newsletter or direct mail, tell them about your organization, its goals, progress toward them and any other events coming up. Depending on the level of donation, you may want to invite some to tours, cultivation events, thank you parties, etc.

Write a Follow-up Plan

No matter what path you take to turn your attendees into supporters, write a plan prior to the event. In the aftermath of an event, with the relief of moving past the event and the need to tend to other demands of your job, it is too easy to forget the follow-up. If you skip this step, you will have kicked away one of the main benefits of hosting an event.

When creating your plan consider:

- How will you decide which communication the attendee will receive? Will you base it on whether she's a first-time attendee or repeat attendee? Whether she made a purchase? And if she did, will you further break it down by the amount?

- Will you communicate via a group email blast, personalized email, letter or phone call?

- What will be included in the message, besides thanks? Possibilities include information about the success of the event or about the organization, the date of the same event next year or the next event your organization will host. How about an invitation to learn more about the organization? Will that be a link to your website, a video or perhaps a one-on-one meeting?

- Who is going to do the communicating? Map out which staff member or volunteer is going to handle each action item.

- When should the communications go out? Set dates and mark them on the calendar. Does an email blast go out the day after the event? Will you make personalized calls within two weeks?

*For a sample of a post-event communications plan, visit **docs.AtoZEventFundraising.com.***

Put your plan down on paper and share it with the staff and volunteers who are helping you implement it. This is the easiest step to skip—but one of the most important ones to focus on after the stage gets cleared away or the traffic cones get picked up. It is much easier (and less expensive) to retain a donor than to find a new one, so consider these attendees part of your stewardship process.

TIP

CHAPTER TO-DO LIST

✔ Choose method(s) of capturing attendee information.

✔ Create a work plan for attendee follow-up.

Part Five

Implementation and Follow-Up of Event Fundraisers

To get your FREE copy of the A-to-Z Guide to Event Fundraising appendix
full of useful tools, checklists, sample document and worksheets, visit
docs.AtoZEventFundraising.com.

CHAPTER

13

STEPS TO EVENT PLANNING

In This Chapter

✔ Choosing the date, time and duration of your event

✔ Selecting a venue

✔ Determining food and beverage needs

✔ Determining parking, security and valet needs

✔ Floor plans

✔ Creating a run-of-show document

✔ Other logistics to consider

✔ Committee meeting planning guide

✔ Event budgets

Since events come in all shapes and sizes, knowing what steps you need to take to ensure success on the big day can be complicated. While this chapter could never cover every step in every circumstance, it should cover most items on your list.

Date, Time and Duration

Choosing when to host your event is one of your biggest decisions. Picking the wrong date can make or break your event. What are the critical things to consider?

Time of year

For some events, there are obvious times of year (e.g., not winter in New England for a golf tournament). For others, it may not be as definite. When selecting the month, consider your average attendee's lifestyle. If you mostly have parents attending, an event during end-of-the-school-year/graduation season may not be the best choice. Try to think through if you were your average guest, how hard would it be to attend. When in doubt, ask a few potential attendees.

Day of the week

For many, Saturday nights are a must. For others, there may be some flexibility. If you are asking chefs to donate their time and services, a Thursday or Sunday may be better as chefs are less likely to leave their restaurants on Fridays and Saturdays. For young families, a Sunday afternoon may be ideal because children are less likely to have other activities.

Other events

For this one, the Internet is your friend. Do a search to find out what events similar to yours (or just likely to appeal to your average attendee) are occurring on the dates you are considering. It's impossible to be the only one hosting an event on any date, but the more you can minimize the competition, the better. If you are hosting a repeat event, did another event bump into yours in a previous year? Don't be afraid to call that organizer to see if she has set a date yet, if you can't find it online. Neither of you wants to compete with the other. If you are in a major city, are there athletic events or concerts on the dates you are considering?

Length of event

When deciding the duration of your event, be sure to budget time for:

- Food and beverage (i.e. How long does it take to serve a four-course dinner?)

- Program (thank-you portion, speakers, awards presentations, anything else?)

- Live auction, paddle raise or silent auction closing activities

- Ample time for people to arrive

- Other activities

Start and stop time

Once you've decided the duration, you can select start and stop times. Don't forget to consider things like traffic, whether dinner is included, and the average person's work schedule if it's a weeknight. (He may want to go home first and change.)

Once you've done your research and decided which time of year and day of the week are best, choose a handful of potential dates. Then you can see what your preferred venue has available. Before making a final decision, check with any guests who must be in attendance to see if those dates are open.

Venue Selection

One of the most important first steps in your planning is choosing a location. Depending on the type of event, this can mean a lot of different things. In general, you want your venue (or event site if it's an outdoor event) to have a few things:

Space

You need to have enough room for the crowd you expect. For a 5K, that means you need to take into account not only the race course itself, but also room for sponsor booths, registration tables, and water and food tables. Don't forget parking: Is there enough for not only your runners and walkers, but sponsors, volunteers, and any spectators? Is the lot used by others at the time you need it? If there isn't enough space, is there another parking lot nearby that you can use? You may need to arrange shuttle buses from that lot.

Rentals

Another important thing to consider when choosing your venue is what is included in your venue fee. Whether you are hosting a golf tournament, a dinner or a 5K, you are going to need items such as tables, chairs and trash cans. You may also need linens, décor, tableware (plates, glassware, flatware), a dance floor, audio/video equipment, internet access and more. Some venues will have these items in-house and will include them in the fee, while others will charge extra for them. You may need to rent them from an outside vendor. No matter what the venue you are considering offers, be sure to find out all the specifics so that you don't have any surprise expenses.

Labor

What is included and what costs extra? Do you have to pay extra for set up and breakdown, bartenders, valet, coat checkers, rest room and general clean-up staff, audio/visual staff, security?

Location

Where is your venue? If most of your supporters are in one part of town, try to select a site close to that area. If you are pulling a crowd from a wide geographical area, is your venue in a central location? Can you get to it fairly easily on the day or night of your event? Or are you making everyone fight traffic? Is there another big event the same day close to your venue that will make it hard to get in and out? The easier you can make it for attendees to get there, the better your turnout will be, especially if there is bad weather.

Restrictions

Does your venue have any restrictions that are deal-breakers? Are you not allowed to have a vehicle in the venue and your biggest sponsor is a dealership that wants to display a car?

Food & Beverage

You probably are going to offer food and beverage, but this can vary from water, bananas and bagels at a 5K to a four-course seated dinner at a gala. When deciding on food and beverage, consider the following:

Who will be providing the food?

For non-athletic events, if you use a hotel, its food and beverage department may require that you purchase the food and beverage from them. If you choose another type of venue, you may be hiring a caterer to provide the food and beverage. Perhaps it's a tasting event and you are recruiting restaurants to host tables that guests will visit for samples. Obviously the more you do yourself, the more complicated it becomes. But doing so may be less expensive, so carefully weigh the pros and cons of each along with the cost when deciding the best option.

If you are providing a dinner

There are numerous ways to serve dinner at an event. Below is some information about the options.

TYPES OF FOOD AND BEVERAGE SERVICE	
Reception or buffet service	Food is arranged on tables, and guests move along the tables and serve themselves; seating can vary from one seat per guest to little or no guest seating; some events also have action, or chef-attended stations, with a chef preparing or serving food, such as an omelet station or meat-carving station.
Plated service	Food is arranged on individual plates and given to guests seated at tables.
Pre-set service	Food is arranged on individual plates and placed on the tables shortly before the guest arrives; this is popular for salad and dessert courses, especially for a luncheon or an event short in duration.
Family style service	Food is served to each table on large platters or in bowls, and guests help themselves and pass to other guests.
Synchronized service	Servers bring an entire table of meals at the same time; for example, a table of ten would have five servers with each bringing two plates; they would surround the table and set the food down at the same time; this is often more expensive than plated service; also called hand service.
Passed service	Servers bring food on trays and offer it to guests to pick up while standing; popular during receptions; also called butlered hors d'oeuvres service

What type of service do you want? Buffet or plated? (Plated is typically less expensive but takes more time.) If seated, how many courses do you want? Appetizer, entrée and dessert? Do you want a salad, cheese course, bread service, something else? Do you want some of the courses pre-set or family style? Are you interested in synchronized service? Passed service for hors d'oeuvres, an hors d'oeuvres display, or none? For some of these options, for example a plated dinner, a tasting of the menu may be offered. What about beverages? Wine and non-alcoholic beverages only at dinner? Open bar or cash bar? Call or premium brands? Your ticket price, program and number of guests all play into these decisions.

For a tasting event

Tasting events are when several chefs (as few as 10, as mant as 100 plus) offer a small tasting to guests. How many chefs do you want? Do you have relationships with them already? Or is this a new event? Are you going to have a VIP area with exclusive chefs or wine? How will beverages be handled? Stations mixed in, or several bars? The number of bars depends on how many guests you expect, with usually one bartender per 75-100 guests, but your venue or caterer can help you. Depending on event flow, you may be better off with several bars spread around with one bartender at each versus only one bar with three or four bartenders. Tasting events come with lots of dirty dishes, or trash if you are using disposable plates and utensils. Be sure to plan ahead on how to manage this – few things are unsightlier than piles of discarded dishes at an event.

For tournaments

Do you want a breakfast buffet for golfers before they tee off? A 19th-hole dinner or awards ceremony when the tournament is over? Both? Is your breakfast a hot buffet with eggs, bacon, sausage, etc. or simply a selection of pastries and bagels? Will the after-meal be casual, such as a catered barbecue, or does your entry fee warrant something more formal like a seated dinner?

For athletic events

You likely need post-race food (water, bananas, bagels, etc.). Do you want anything else? Would hot food make your race more attractive to a runner deciding between yours and another?

Food and beverage often has additional costs that are easy to forget. Remember to find out how your venue or caterer manages:

Labor

This is a huge one. Service for a seated dinner (although built into the meal price), often costs more than for a buffet since it takes multiple servers to keep a large room served and clean. You may also have other labor expenses such as bartenders, chef-attended stations, cleaning staff (e.g., checking restrooms and emptying trash cans if you have a tasting event), in-house-required security, etc.

Other food expenses

While it's a given you will pay for food and beverage; some caterers or venues will impose other charges. Do you have to pay for ice? (A big foodie event requires large quantities to keep beverages cold.) Tasting events may incur extra costs for trash and recycling cans. Are there costs for cleanup, set up, anything else? If you get donated wine or other alcoholic beverages, is there a corkage fee?

Non-food expenses

Do you have to pay extra for tables, chairs, linens, chair covers, and simple décor (e.g., votive candles)?

Parking, Security & Valet

It is easy to overlook parking, security and valet, so be sure to think about the following:

Safety

The safety of guests, vendors and staff must be a top priority. You may need to hire off-duty police to help runners get across busy intersections during a 5K or to guide drivers exiting the parking garage after your gala.

Parking

Plan to have ample parking for your guests, sponsors, volunteers and vendors. If they have to pay to park, will you cover the cost for all or some of these people? If so, can you get it donated or at a discount? If you aren't covering the cost of parking (especially for volunteers), you need to be upfront about the cost and distance from the event.

Valet

Should you hire valet for your high-end event? It's a nice feature, but it can be logistically difficult and expensive, so do your research. If your guests will leave at one time, it may be difficult for a valet to retrieve cars quickly. In addition, if the parking spots the valet uses aren't isolated from the others, the valets may be stuck in the same exit lines as paying guests. No matter what your parking situation is, do everything possible to make it easy for guests to leave. Have multiple exit lanes and advance payment (so guests don't have to wait while everyone feeds a credit card to the machine at the exit). Another option: Include the parking fee in the event ticket cost. Remember that the parking garage is the final impression your guest will have of your event, so you want to make it as positive as possible.

Security

Things of value that are unwatched at an event do get stolen, or mistakenly taken. You may have a very valuable auction item or gift bags. So it might be wise to hire an off-duty policeman or a security guard. Sometimes a volunteer can do the job.

Floor Plan

Floor plans are an important part of any event. These drawings of your event space with all the items you plan to have in the venue (or outside) are an extremely important planning tool. So what should the drawings include?

Tables and chairs

This may be as simple as nine round tables with ten chairs and a head table of ten, for a total of 100 guests. Or the plan may be more complicated, with tasting table stations (often with a front and back table so the chefs have a prep area), auction tables, registration tables, bars, cocktail high tops (smaller, higher tables without chairs where guests can set drinks and food plates), and more. Your floor plan (usually created by your venue or caterer with your input) will be your key to everything from guest seating to helping you determine how many tables, linens and floral arrangements you need.

Stage

Does your event have a stage? If so, be sure to include that in your floor plan along with specifics about its size. Consider also what type of entrance you want to the stage. Do you want steps on both sides, one side or in the center?

Do you need a railing or ADA ramp? (For more information about American Disabilities Act requirements for events, ask your event planner, venue or visit https://adata.org/publication/temporary-events-guide). If you are using a podium, do you want one with a microphone, or do you need a handheld or lavalier (clip-on) microphone?

Water and electricity

Any water or electrical needs should also be clearly marked on your floor plan. Power can be tricky because some items take more **TIP** power than others. For example, items that heat up such as cook-ing surfaces need more power than an average plug. So be sure you tell the venue contact what you are plugging in so she can accommodate it. In some cases, you may need to modify your original floor plan so that you have access to water or power where you need it. Be aware that some venues will charge extra for this.

Real World Example:

At a tasting event, a restaurant chef arrived with an ice cream maker that took more than the traditional 120-volt plug. The organization and A/V company were forced to react quickly to accommodate the chef. A quick change in floor plan, along with running some additional electrical wires, fixed the problem. Lesson learned: Be sure to ask any vendors their electrical needs ahead of time to avoid last-minute changes.

Fire safety

Most venues have strict rules to ensure guest and staff safety if there is a fire. Your venue will know all the specifics, but in gen- **TIP** eral, you must provide enough space for smooth traffic flow, and you may not block exits. So not only can you not put a table directly in front of a door, but you also can't put a table in the direct path that a person would take to get to that door. If your venue requires a fire inspection, ask for it as early in the day as possible so if you must make changes to your floor plan, you have time to do so before guests arrive.

Rest rooms

Are your rest rooms easy to find? Do you need signs to help direct guests? Does your venue do periodic checks to make sure the rest rooms stay clean? If you are outdoors, do you need portable rest rooms? Will port-a-potties work, or do you need larger or nicer ones? When deciding how many port-a-potties to rent, consider your expected turnout, the length of event, whether there will be more women than men, and if you are serving food and/or alcohol.

Real World Example:

At one black-tie event, the organizer went into the rest room at the end of the event. She found not only numerous wine glasses and other debris on the floor, but a volunteer's daytime clothes hanging on the back of one of the stall doors. Ask if your venue has a staff member checking the rest rooms for cleanliness. If not, designate a volunteer to monitor the rest rooms and alert a venue staff member when they need cleaning.

Details

Do you need a registration table, media check-in table, a VIP area, a coat check, or a room where special guests can wait or be interviewed? If you need to organize registration or auction checkout lines or certain areas are going to be off-limits to guests during all or some of the event, you may need **rope and stanchion**. Do you need trash cans, recycling bins or places for dirty plates to be set? All these things should be carefully considered and put on your floor plan.

rope and stanchion: flexible ropes, often made of velvet, and moveable posts that the ropes affix to, which allow you to control lines or keep guests in or out of certain areas

Run of Show

Each event needs a run of show, or a document that lists everything that should happen at the event with corresponding times. This document tells organizational staff and volunteers, as well as venue employees, what should be happening and when. Run of shows should contain:

Deliveries and pick-ups

Anything that will be delivered or picked up for the event should be listed along with who is bringing it, what it is and the estimated arrival time.

Detailed list of what is happening at the event and when

Anything that is happening at your event should be documented with a time, location (if it's not obvious), and a staff member or volunteer who will be in charge of that portion of the event. The list includes event start times, stage presentations, live auctions, silent auction closures and awards presentations. Don't forget items such as when doors should be opened and by whom and any switching of signs (e.g., welcome on the way in, thanks for coming on the way out).

Staff, volunteer and important guest arrival times

Who is coming, when, and what are their main responsibilities.

Organizational staff, venue staff and volunteer list

A quick reference chart with all key people, their contact information including cell phone, and their assignment is a must.

Vendor list with contact information

It is helpful to have your vendor list on hand in case something doesn't arrive or arrives incorrectly.

Task list

Having a list of tasks that need to be done before, during and after the event can be very helpful. Event days are full of questions, so the more you can spell out what needs to be done, and when, the more self-sufficient volunteers and staff members can be.

Your run of show is easily your most important document on event day. It should contain all your event's most important information and should guide everyone helping that day as you orchestrate a smooth and successful event. You will use this document to communicate with everyone involved.

For influencers in attendance, such as honorary chairs, you can edit the run of show to include just the larger aspects of your event, contact information for one or two persons should the **TIP** influencer need anything, as well as specifics on where that person needs to be and when (e.g. for a check-presentation photo). Provide each special guest a copy, but also print and bring additional copies in case any of these guests arrives without her copy.

Miscellaneous

Event details are nearly never-ending. Here are a few more things to think about during your planning:

A/V (audio & visual) needs

This can be one of your largest expenses. When planning, divide your A/V needs into "must have" and "like to have" categories. If you are doing a stage presentation, you will likely need lighting, sound and potentially video. How many screens do you need, if any? Do you need radios to communicate with each other? What about microphones? Is one on the podium enough, or do you need a handheld, clip-on lavalier or headset? If you have a band, do you need anything special for them? Are you doing a **live camera feed**? PowerPoint presentation? Will you use a **gobo** that has your organization's or a sponsor's logo? Do you need to hire or find a volunteer stage manager? All of these items should be thought through and priced before you make final decisions. If you aren't sure if an item is worth the expense, ask yourself: "Will having this help me raise more money?"

live camera feed: when a camera man follows the main stage events so they can be projected onto large screens so guests can easily see what is happening on stage from all parts of the venue

gobo: a template inserted in front of a light that allows a logo or other information to be projected onto a wall, the floor or another surface

Load-in and load-out

How will you and your vendors bring auction items, food, signs, and everything else into the venue? Can you park near the front door and bring items in on carts? Or do you have to use a loading dock? Can you load items in the day prior? Do you have enough volunteers to help? How about load-out? Same way? Be sure this has been thought through, especially if guests and vendors will be leaving at the same time. A single elevator to a parking garage can be a huge bottleneck, so provide extra volunteers to help manage it.

TIP

Transportation

Will guests or special guests need transportation? Do you have enough golf carts for a golf tournament? Do event emcees or speakers need car service to and from the airport, their home or hotel? Is it a long walk to your event entrance so you need transportation for guests who have trouble walking? If there is not enough parking near your race starting line, do you need a shuttle bus to transport athletes and others? If your finish line is far away from parking, do you need to provide transportation back to the parking area or post-race party? If you do need transportation for your guests, be sure to let them know where to pick it up and where it will drop them off via pre-event communications (emails, letters with tickets, etc.) and via signs at the event.

Décor

This can easily become the runaway train of your budget if you aren't careful. Florals, specialty linens or chairs, etc. can quickly add up to a lot of money without adding much revenue potential. Choosing a theme for your event is often fun and can freshen up an event that has been around for several years. But be careful it doesn't end up costing too much. Some ways to save? Consider linens that the venue provides at no extra charge **TIP** for areas that aren't as visible (or covered with dinnerware) and pay for something fancier at highly seen areas, such as the registration table. Same for florals: A great eye-catching floral on the way into the event may be worth the investment. Meanwhile, save money by using smaller vases with a few elegant loose flowers and some votive candles for guest tables.

Signs

No matter what type of event you are hosting, you will likely need signs. Categories include welcome, impact (what you are raising **TIP** money for, information about the problem your organization is working to solve), directional (entrance, rest rooms, race start, silent auction, etc.), sponsors, timing (start time for 5K, onstage sign that states when the program and/or live auction begins) and exit (thank you for attending, show receipt for paid auction items, save the date for next year, parking fees paid and/or valet). When planning your signs, see if there are signs that can be reused from year to year (or event to event) to save money. Be sure to also budget holders for the signs; some venues provide them, but you may need to rent or buy easels if you have a large quantity. If you have an outdoor event, have a plan for keeping signs in place during wind or other weather conditions. Depending on the size and type of event you are having, sign management can be a great job for a volunteer (e.g., creating a spreadsheet of what is needed, proofreading, working with the vendor, picking them up). No matter who manages the signs, be sure to proofread them carefully at least a few days prior to the event, if possible. That way if you discover any errors, you will have time to get the signs reprinted.

Entertainment

Are you planning to have a band, DJ or speaker? When hiring entertainers, think about what your needs are. Do you want people to dance? Is the music more audio wallpaper, a soothing sound that people can talk over easily? If you need an emcee, a DJ may be better than a band. When you book your entertainment, find out not only the cost, but any expectations. Do the musicians require food and beverage throughout the night? The same meal as the guests, or a boxed meal? What are their break requirements? What happens when they aren't playing? Do they need a special dressing room? What are their electrical requirements? Can they meet your load-in and load-out requirements and sound-check time? Stage requirements? Do they need all their own sound equipment or will they need some from the venue? How will they work with you and your program? Do they have special parking or meal requirements?

Printed items

In addition to signs, you may need other printed items, including marketing flyers, registration forms, and medals or trophies. Food and beverage events may have save-the-date cards with envelopes, invitations with envelopes, programs, tickets, menus and more. This is another great job for a volunteer to manage.

Photographer

Would a photographer be helpful at your event? If you want to seek media coverage after your event, try to line up a photographer and photographer's assistant (to capture names of people in the photos—a great volunteer job!). You can also use the photos as part of the next year's sponsor-solicitation materials, or as part of thank you letters to guests or volunteers.

Tent

If your event is outdoors, you may need a tent. Be sure to think carefully about your floor plan and traffic flow when deciding on the size, shape and location of your tent. If it rains, will the area become muddy so you should consider getting flooring? What about temperature – is heat or air conditioning needed? Get at least two quotes because not only are you likely to receive different prices, but one vendor may have creative tenting ideas that could improve the event flow, or save expenses.

Insurance and permits

What type of insurance do you need? Most venues require you to carry at least some sort of liability insurance (or show proof that your organization has it), and you may require additional insurance if you're serving alcohol. You may also need permits if you are doing an outdoor event, using public roads or receiving donated alcohol. Be sure to do your homework so you are covered if something unforeseen occurs. Ensure that you have all permits that you need so your event can't be closed down.

Committee Meetings

When planning your event, it's also important to meet with your committee and work with its members to reach your goals. Below is a suggested meeting schedule and what to do during these meetings.

When To Meet	Who To Invite	Information Covered
At least 6 months before event	Full committed committee; any potential committee members	Basic event overview (who, what, where, when); introduction of committee chairs and quick overview of committee; event goals; schedule of meetings; committees that need additional members; organizational overview (either complete if new committee, or updates since previous year for veteran committees)
Monthly meetings (suggested 2 - 6 months before event)	Full committee	Overview of status of event (sponsors, auction, ticket sales, etc.); logistics update; committee chairs report on progress and where help is needed
2 months before event (suggested every 2 weeks)	Committee chairs	Overview of status of event (sponsors, auction, ticket sales, etc.); logistics update; committee chairs report on progress and where help is needed
1 - 2 weeks prior to event	Full committee	Go through complete run of show document so as many people as possible are aware of what is supposed to happen; assign committee members tasks
Auction Committee meeting (2-3 weeks out)	Auction Committee members and day-of volunteers	Training for auction
Stage manager or race director meeting (1-2 weeks out)	Stage manager or race director, committee members in charge of logistics	Go through run of show in entirety for stage manager or race director
Auctioneer meeting (2-3 weeks out; potentially earlier if using your auctioneer to help order items for printed program)	Live auctioneer, volunteers managing live auction, committee chair	Go through live auction items to inform auctioneer and answer questions. Be sure to let him/her know of any minimums or consignment values; providing equivalencies for typical auction bump-up levels is also helpful. (See Chapter 11.)

When To Meet	Who To Invite	Information Covered
Post-event meeting	Full committee	Review what went well, what could be improved and anything else you want to remember for the following year. Despite being tired, try to have this meeting quickly after the event while memories are freshest.

Budgets

It is important to create a budget and to use it as you make decisions so that you have ample profit, making your organization's time and effort worthwhile.

Most events are considered successful if expenses are less than 30 percent of the revenue produced. The ideal is 10-15 percent, but this can be difficult, especially for new events. When creating a budget, get estimates for all the items you may need. From there, it is a good idea to create a good, better and best-case scenario for revenue. Try to track your break-even point on the event, as well as any fixed and variable costs, along with what expenses are mandatory even if you have to cancel the event. (To download a sample budget, visit docs.AtoZEventFundraising.com.)

CHAPTER TO-DO LIST

- ✔ Choose date, time and duration of your event.

- ✔ Select venue.

- ✔ Determine any food and beverage, parking, security or valet needs.

- ✔ Create floor plan.

- ✔ Create run of show document.

- ✔ Plan committee meetings, basic agendas and inform committee of dates.

- ✔ Create a budget with good, better and best-case revenue scenarios. Keep it updated throughout the event planning process.

CHAPTER

14

PRE- AND POST-EVENT WEEK

In This Chapter

- ✔ What to do the week prior to the event

- ✔ Event-day checklist

- ✔ Week-after-the-event follow-up items

After all your hard work and planning, it's finally the week of the event! Use this guide to ensure everything runs smoothly during the days prior to the event, at the event itself and during the few days following.

The Week Prior to the Event

The week of the event has finally arrived, and you are ready to put all your plans into action. Here are some additional tips to ensure a smooth event:

Confirm vendors

Three to five business days before the event, confirm all vendors and delivery times. Unless you've booked a vendor within a week or two of the event, you should call or email each one to confirm what has been ordered, the delivery date and time, and any other delivery information needed (e.g., location of loading dock, how item should be labeled if going to a hotel). Keep track of who has confirmed and re-call or email any that haven't until you reach all vendors. Such confirmations can help prevent event-day disasters. In addition, prepare any payments due to vendors and pack them where they can be easily found on event day.

Venue check-in

By now you should have had a final run of show meeting with your venue, but if you haven't, you should do so. Also, if you are expecting any deliveries to the venue prior to the day of the event, check to see that they have all arrived. If you did have a final meeting, check in one or two days before the event to provide any changes or updates that would affect the venue staff.

Tickets/participants

If your event has tickets, by now all attendees should have them. If they don't, you will need to set up a will-call area and have their tickets in envelopes with their names, filed alphabetically for quick check-in. If your event doesn't have tickets, a day or so prior to the event you will need to print an attendee list for check-in staff to use. It is helpful to print multiple copies and sometimes, if you have a large corporate attendance, to print both an alphabetical list of individuals by last name as well as a list of companies with their allotted seats (and guest names if you have them). Many auction software programs also include a guest/table management system. For athletic events, this is the time to do last-minute organizing of race numbers and anything else a participant may get the day of the race (first aid items, safety pins, cash box for walk-in registrations, T-shirt, goody bag assembly, etc.).

Gift or goody bags

Assemble these bags ahead of time. If you have an evening event with a full day of set up, it can be easier to assemble your bags onsite with help from day-of-event volunteers. To simplify the process, give volunteers a list of exactly what each bag should contain. You should also clearly mark all four sides of each box that contains gift bag items (e.g., GIFT BAGS – flashlights – 1/bag). This will allow volunteers to put the bags together with little or no guidance from you, freeing you up for more important tasks. If you have an early morning event, you will probably want to assemble the bags a day or two ahead. Be sure to think about where they will be stored at the event and how to transport them; they can take up more room than you would think!

Sponsor activations

If your event has sponsors that will be participating at the event (e.g., hosting a booth, providing an attendee experience), check in with them a few days prior to the event to ensure that they are ready. Provide information regarding parking, load-in, load-out, dress codes, security of valuables, etc. If there is anything special they need from the venue (electricity, water, etc.), be sure the venue knows this and can accommodate them.

Auctions

The week prior to the event can be frantic as you pick up items, complete data entry and print display and/or bid sheets. Having multiple volunteers to help with what may seem like an endless list of tasks helps make it go smoothly both before and during the event. This is also a good time to write up any instructions for volunteers the day of the event, if you haven't already.

Media

If your event has media as special guests, not only should you reach out to confirm their attendance, but also provide any pertinent information such as dress code, parking, location and timing of any interviews.

Volunteers

Reconfirm your volunteers' attendance and roles at the event. Using online sources such as SignUpGenius.com or VolunteerSpot.com is an easy way for people to sign up and for you to send reminders and information. Volunteers with more complicated roles may need training a couple of weeks prior to the event. Volunteers with simple jobs can receive training (verbal and/or written) the day of the event, but be sure to schedule it and tell your volunteers when and where they need to be. For those volunteers with moderately complicated tasks, email training information before the event to give them time to read it and ask questions. All volunteers should receive clear communications about your expectations as well as information on dress code, parking, arrival time, where to place valuables, whether food and beverage will be provided, departure times and check-out procedures (e.g., whether they need to check out to get a free parking pass). If you are providing food for your volunteers, be sure to order it and arrange pickup or delivery, if needed. Remember, recruiting more volunteers than needed is a must because you will always lose a few the couple days leading up to the event.

Audio/video

If your event has a lot of audio and video, send your presentations and any videos you are showing to the A/V company several days prior to the event. Different types of computers or screen sizes can cause presentations to appear differently, so it is wise to test **everything** in advance. If there are multiple presentations or videos, prepare an A/V event flow, which tells the A/V manager what needs to be shown and when. Include not only file names and specific times, but any notes that will make things run as you would like them to. For example, if you show photos of your honorary chairperson during your stage presentation, you may have a note that says: "Approximately 8 p.m. – Honorary Chairperson Lisa Smith welcomes guests -show page 1 of Stage.PPT when she enters the stage." For complicated programs, it can help to meet with the A/V manager before or during event day to walk through it with him. This is another great place for a volunteer.

Signs and printed materials

Pick up programs, signs and any other printed materials a day or two prior to your event, if possible. This will give you time to make any corrections or to print additional items.

Run of show documents and scripts

Send these to appropriate people along with pertinent information, such as parking, dress code, etc.

Look book

It is often helpful to create a look book with pictures and descriptions of key attendees. This is especially useful if an important person from your organization is attending and doesn't know everyone. Include special guests, key sponsors, media, local influencers, key volunteers, etc. with both a picture and their role with the organization.

Print outs

Since printing can be difficult on event day, any documents you've sent out should be printed and filed. It is not uncommon for a special guest to forget his script, volunteers to need floor plans, and venue staff to need event flows. Make multiple copies and staple one marked "original" into each file. Place them in a central, easy-to-find location on event day so you can direct people to help themselves. Also, if your event has a complicated set-up, print one very large copy of your floor plan and display it on an easel in a central spot.

Pack event materials.

All events have some materials that will be used for set up. It could be frames for silent auction signs, props, gift bag items, awards, vendor payments or other items. To ensure an easy load-in, be sure to mark the boxes with your event materials clearly with their contents, ideally on all four sides. If materials need to be delivered to different parts of the venue, mark that on the boxes as well.

Assign "go to" people.

If you are the main event organizer, it will be helpful if you assign co-captains to all or part of your event. Having multiple people to make decisions can be extremely helpful.

An email of thanks and encouragement to your committee and volunteers

A quick email the day before the event thanking them for all their work (so far and to come) can go a long way.

During the Event

Finally! Event day has arrived! Use this checklist to help ensure a smooth and profitable event.

Athletic Events

☐ Pick up ice, if needed.

☐ Make sure the event is set up according to your plan.

☐ Post signs.

☐ Organize registration table, including cash box for walk-in registrations.

☐ Organize goody bags.

☐ Test PA/communication system.

☐ Assemble start/finish area.

☐ Place course signs and/or cones where needed.

☐ Set up food and beverage, on-course water stations and trash cans.

☐ Train race course volunteers and assign them their locations.

- ☐ Set up awards.

- ☐ Set up first aid station.

- ☐ Post-race cleanup, including picking up signs

Golf Tournaments

- ☐ Check to ensure the event is set up according to your floor plan.

- ☐ Post signs in entry area.

- ☐ Organize registration table.

- ☐ Organize gifts, awards, prizes and sponsor-appreciation gifts.

- ☐ Test PA/communication system.

- ☐ Set up auction area, if needed.

- ☐ Place sponsor signs on course.

- ☐ Set up food and beverage.

- ☐ Train course volunteers; assign course placement.

- ☐ Ensure carts are organized and ready for golfers.

- ☐ Organize on-course contests.

- ☐ Post-event cleanup

Food and Beverage Events

- ☐ Make sure vendors have delivered everything.

- ☐ Make sure the event is set up according to your floor plan.

- ☐ Set up auction and test auction payment process.

- ☐ Organize registration, media check-in, coat check.

- ☐ Organize gift bags.

- ☐ Place any printed materials such as signs, programs, table signs, place cards, etc.

- ☐ Test audio/video and run through program.

- ☐ Fire inspection, if needed

- ☐ Entertainment sound check

- ☐ Ensure all important guests, speakers, auctioneer, etc. have arrived.

- ☐ Train volunteers and assign them to their places.

- ☐ Store any items not needed during the event or if needed during the event, ensure volunteers know where they can be found for replenishment (e.g., extra disposable forks and plates at a tasting event).

- ☐ Post-event cleanup.

Once your guests have arrived, it is time to follow your run-of-show and watch all your months of hard work start to pay off. At this point, you need to trust that you did all you, your staff and volunteers could to make your event a success. Stay calm, keep a watch that key moments go as planned and have a successful fundraising event.

If something does not go according to plan, take a deep breath and don't panic. Think through best remedies and take action. Most important, whenever possible, keep things smooth for your guests and sponsors. Every event has its hiccup, but good event planners manage them calmly and most often, guests aren't aware that things may not be happening as planned. At the end of the event, take a deep breath and know you have done a great thing to help advance your cause and organization.

Real World Example:

The morning of the event, the chairperson did a walk-through of the venue. Despite approving the floor plan previously, he had several changes he insisted needed to be made. The event director politely tried to convince the chairperson that the original (approved) floor plan was best and why, but the chairperson continued to insist on the changes. Thankfully, the venue staff was flexible and made the changes as requested. The event was not noticeably effected, and despite a bit of unnecessary stress, the rest of the event went as planned.

Post-Event Activities

Hooray! Your event is over and, no doubt, a great success! Although it's tempting to take a few days off to rest, there are several important details that should be taken care of sooner rather than later.

As Soon as Possible, After the Event

Call auction winners who haven't paid for their items.

If any silent auction winners haven't paid, call them as soon as possible, ideally a day or two after the event. The more time that goes by, the more likely you will not receive return calls.

Thank your volunteers.

A quick email to thank your volunteers and committees for their hard work with an overview of the success you had is a great spirit-builder. For some volunteers, such as committee chairs, sending a small gift is appropriate. If you've scheduled your post-event meeting or thank you get-together, let them know the time, date and location.

Send press release.

Within 24 hours, send a press release to local media with results and photos.

A Week or Two after the Event

Financial reconciliations

Once you have completed mission-critical tasks, it's time to analyze event finances. Analyze your different revenue streams (sponsorship, ticket sales, auction and other) both against budget and previous years. Make notes about how you could improve. If any sponsorships, donations or auction items are unpaid, make notes and take action to collect payments.

Post-event meeting

Host a post-event meeting with your committee and volunteers to discuss what to start, stop and continue next year.

Thank you letters

Send thank you letters to sponsors (including a recap with amount raised, media highlights and any other accomplishments), volunteers and others who helped make the event possible. Include a personalized note from you, or the event chair, if possible.

Acknowledgement letters

Send letters to all donors, including live and silent auction donors, and guests who purchased live or silent auction items or made any other type of donation at the event.

Post-event cultivation

Connect with event attendees, sponsors or volunteers who showed an extended interest in your organization. Look for opportunities to create new volunteers, donors and supporters. (See Chapter 12.)

CHAPTER TO-DO LIST

- ✔ **Work through items on pre-event list in this chapter.**

- ✔ **On event day, work through your event type's checklist.**

- ✔ **Plan and implement post-event activities.**

POST-EVENT ANALYSIS

In This Chapter

- ✔ Post-event committee meeting

- ✔ When to retire or remake an event

- ✔ When to consider hiring a professional event planner

Once event day is over and you have all the post-event cleanup done, it's tempting to put your event behind you and look to the next project. Don't. You would miss a valuable opportunity to learn what went well, what could be improved upon and what should stay the same.

Post-Event Meetings

Probably the best way to analyze your event's strong and weak points is a meeting of your staff and committee chairs and/or committee members. The meeting should be held within three or four weeks so it is fresh in everyone's memory. When you send a thank you email the day after the event, ask volunteers and committee members to jot down their thoughts about what went well or could be improved while it's fresh in their minds. Committee members can bring those notes to the meeting or, if unable to attend, share them via email or phone. For stage managers, auctioneers, etc., a quick one-on-one meeting or phone conversation works well since their jobs are specialized.

The post-event meeting should include:

Thank you

First and foremost, this meeting should begin with a heartfelt thank you for all the hard work that was done both on behalf of you, your organization and the people or things that it serves.

Results

Share any information about how the event did. Do you know gross revenue, percentage of expenses, or how the sponsorships, auctions or ticket sales/registrations did this year compared to last? Do you have an estimate of how much the event raised overall? How many new supporters have you added to your database? Did you identify people who could potentially be a big help to your organization?

What went well

Ask meeting attendees to identify successes before and during the event. This is a perfect opportunity to brag about the committee chairs and members who worked hard and did a great job. It's also a time to discuss any improvements that were made and whether they achieved their goals.

The challenges for next time

What does your committee think needs to be improved? As a leader, identify problems you saw, explain the likely causes and offer thoughts on how to eliminate them. Taking responsibility for problems, where appropriate, is important.

Anything you should start, stop or continue that wasn't already identified

This is the same information as above, but asking it in a different way will often bring out new information.

Discussion of your next event or the next time you do this event

The post-event meeting is a great time to assess the interest of current committee members and volunteers to continue to help if you do the event the following year, or with other events your organization may be hosting. This should be a soft ask, but it's a good way to get a read on recruitment priorities for the following year.

When to Retire or Remake an Event

What happens if the event doesn't turn out as you'd hoped? How do you decide if it just needs to be freshened up or if it should be retired? Here are a few things to consider:

Net profit

The bottom line of any fundraiser should be: Did it make money? If you lost money, you need to carefully analyze why. Did you sell fewer tickets than expected? If so, why? Is it something that is likely to change? (Maybe it rained at your 5K, so you had no walk–ups.) Or was it something less likely to change such as lacking the list capacity to make the event break even? How old is your event? If it's your first year and you didn't make money, but came close and had other positive benefits (new supporters, more awareness, etc.), it may be worth giving it at least one more year to see if it can be profitable.

Time investment

Even if your event was profitable, what was your staff time investment? Did two full-time people work almost exclusively on the event for several months? What else could they do with that time? Would it be better to invest their time in increasing individual giving? Applying for grants? Something else?

Other benefits

What other benefits did your organization receive? Did you expand your database significantly? Did people approach you wanting to be more involved as volunteers, donors or sponsors? While the fundraising aspect of the event is extremely important, it isn't the only measure of success, especially for a new event.

Events can be challenging and often don't succeed in every aspect. When looking at whether to continue or suspend an event, look objectively at the challenges and figure out if they can be overcome. If you do decide to repeat the event, set up milestones at key decision points to help you decide if you should abandon the event or go through with it for the following year.

When To Hire Help

Many events use paid help or event planning companies. Here are a few things to consider in deciding if you should hire someone:

Profitability

If your event is profitable and has lots of components, it may be time to hire help. While many organizations don't want to pay part of their event proceeds to a planner or event management company, it is often worth the investment. Planners can give you back staff time that can be used to help raise funds in other ways. Also, planners are experts at what they do. They often have ideas that save money or bring in more revenue. Some planners even have relationships with vendors that may cut expenses. (For example, a planner with a relationship with a linen company may be able to share a 10% vendor discount). In addition, event companies can sometimes provide equipment that you would have to rent otherwise (e.g., a start/finish line and cones for a road race).

Knowledge

Depending on the type of event, especially if it's a first-time event, it may be well worth the money to hire a planner because of her knowledge. If you've never planned a 5K, the rules of the road and city and county permitting requirements can be daunting, and if not complied with, costly. Hosting a battle of the bands? Has anyone on your staff or volunteer committee ever done something like that? If not, it may be wise to bring on someone who has.

Time-intensive activities

Certain parts of an event eat up a lot of time. Even if you don't have the budget to hire a full-time planner, it is often worth it to find a person to help with some of the time-intensive, but necessary, tasks if you don't have a volunteer to take them on. A good example is the silent auction. Do all the items need to be put into a database so you can print bid sheets, etc.? Or put into the auction software? Do you have someone who can send out tickets on a daily basis as the event approaches?

If you are considering hiring help, it doesn't have to be all or nothing. Some events are big, and hiring a company to handle most of the details is a sound investment. Other times you may just need someone who will put in 10-20 hours per week during the final 6-8 weeks. No matter what you decide, be sure to get a full understanding of what the person will do for you. Some planners will literally do it all with your guidance—sponsor solicitation, sponsor activations, silent auction, logistics including floor plan, rentals and more. Some can even provide staff so you don't need as many volunteers. Other planners will handle only certain parts, either because of your budget constraints or because they lack the expertise. Shop around and get a detailed quote with the project scope. Ask for references or question those the planner has worked with previously to be sure the person or company you choose is the right one.

CHAPTER TO-DO LIST

✔ Host a meeting with your committee; note 3-5 action items for the following year that will improve your event the most.

✔ Analyze results to help you decide if the event needs to stay the same, be remade or even retired.

✔ For profitable, but time-intensive, events, consider hiring a planner.

CONCLUSION

Wow! As *The A-to-Z Guide to Event Fundraising* demonstrates, there are many factors involved in organizing a successful event fundraiser. In the book's early chapters, you discovered the basics about event fundraising and by now, you should have used the extensive list of fundraising events, and its corresponding advice, to help you choose the event that will bring your organization the most success.

Revenue

Event ***sponsorships*** are the bread and butter of event fundraising and with the information included about who to approach to be a sponsor, necessary components of your sponsor proposal, determining sponsor levels (including benefits and pricing) and how to ensure your sponsors come back year after year, you are bound to have success. You are also ready to maximize the second most common revenue stream, ***participant fees***, after reading the how-to guides on pricing your tickets, determining the maximum number of tickets you can sell and tactics on how to achieve a sell-out. ***Live, silent and online auctions*** are explained from start to finish including how to solicit items, what sells the best and even the most minute logistical details of running the auction. Decision factors concerning which auctions, if any, to have at your event, as well as other revenue producing ideas are offered to help you decide which components to include in your event *The A-to-Z Guide to Event Fundraising* even provided you a way to increase revenue for your organization via partial or full in-kind donations.

Supporters

As you know, it can take a village to organize a successful fundraising event so we've provided guidance on how best to use your human capital. Whether you're recruiting members of your **board of directors** to help you attract new sponsors or serve as committee members, or **volunteers** helping out for a few hours at the event, you are armed with check lists to keep you organized and make the most of your help. You even know how to engage other community members to participate in your event to increase its appeal to guests or sponsors. **Public relations** is another key component of event success. Our start-to-finish guide to garner public relations has you covered, helping you to not only sell tickets to your event, but increase public awareness of your organization and create further reach for your sponsors. Or, if time is short for you, you have the bare bones approach to PR so you don't miss out on this important opportunity.

Creating Lasting Impact

Part of why you chose to host an event, versus another fundraising method, is that it provides you the amazing ability to create a new set of organizational supporters or encourage existing supporters to move to a deeper level of involvement. *The A-to-Z Guide to Event Fundraising* has provided tools to help you unlock the secrets of creating this loyalty by showing attendees your **organization's impact**, both before and during the event. You are now empowered with what you need to know to ensure **continued communication and relationship-building** with your attendees after the event ends.

Implementation and Follow-Up

You have a guide for the **planning and logistics** of your event. Where to host your event, what to consider when making important decisions about food, beverage, parking, security and more – you've got it covered! You know about creating your floor plan, event schedule, committee meeting schedule, as well as how to generate, maintain and keep within a budget. Check lists to use before and during the event will make it as smooth and stress-free as possible, while ensuring you don't miss anything important. Through post-event analysis, you will know how to make your next event even better, if you should consider hiring paid help, discontinuing or even reinventing your event.

Our downloadable appendix (available at *docs.AtoZEventFundraising.com*) has given you the useful tools, checklists, sample documents and worksheets to help you stay organized and keep track of your event details. Along with this guide, these documents will take you, step by step, from the day-one decision-making moments to the completion of the event (and beyond!).

One Final Note

While the key planning and logistical information provided in this book is important, it is purposefully placed near the end. What you learned in the first twelve chapters of *The A-to-Z Guide to Event Fundraising* is what differentiates your *fundraising* event from every other event. Your event needs to run smooth for both participants and sponsors, but just as important, it needs to raise revenue and engage the community. *Our biggest piece of advice:* Don't focus on the planning and logistics to the extent that you forego the most important benefits - raising revenue and enlarging your supporter base. This is often harder than it may appear. It will take conscious effort and planning to not be swallowed up by the "must be attended to" event details, but you can do it!

Congratulations!

Whether you read this book from cover to cover, or only select chapters where you need guidance, we are sure you will help your event reach new heights. Hats off to you, your work and commitment to raise funds for your non-profit's important mission. Your role in making your community a better place is important, so thank you for all you do.

Best wishes for a highly profitable and successful event!

ABOUT THE AUTHOR

Amy S. Crowell, CFRE

Photo: Heidi Geldhauser

Amy Crowell, founder of Next Stage Advisors, has more than two decades of experience in nonprofit management, fundraising, marketing and sales, event management, and strategic and financial planning. She has overseen numerous nonprofit fundraisers, including grassroots campaigns, small and large events and national multimillion-dollar corporate-sponsored programs.

Amy helps nonprofits of all sizes meet and beat their fundraising goals via event consulting, board development, grant writing and more.

Prior to founding Next Stage Advisors, Amy was a leader at Share Our Strength No Kid Hungry, a national nonprofit, where she raised more than $3 million via events and donations. She also led Share Our Strength's grassroots fundraising and youth engagement efforts, building a community of people of all ages to help spread the word and raise funds to end childhood hunger. Previously, she was marketing director for Fifth Group Restaurants of Atlanta.

She holds a B.S. in business from the University of Connecticut and an MBA from Brenau University. She is a Certified Fund Raising Executive, Certified Public Accountant and a member of the Association of Fundraising Professionals and Les Dames d'Escoffier International. Amy enjoys travel and exploring anything related to food and beverages. She lives with her husband and three children outside of Atlanta.

For more information about how Next Stage Advisors can help your nonprofit reach its next stage of success, visit NextStageAdv.com or contact Next Stage Advisors at 770.609.7188 or amy@nextstageadv.com.

**Allison Palestrini, author of Chapter 10 –
The Role of Public Relations**

Photo: Heidi Geldhauser

Founder of Type A Development, a partnership and communications consulting company, Allison spent ten years in the food and lifestyle industry—most recently as Southeast director for the nonprofit Share Our Strength—pairing her passion for the culinary world with her professional acumen to offer frank, straightforward, no-nonsense advice that achieves results. Allison's expertise makes her a natural to help with public relations, fundraising, event sponsorship sales, viability studies, and, in every case, connect brands with best-fit audiences and influencers. She holds a B.A. in journalism (public relations) from the University of Georgia and is a member of Les Dames d'Escoffier International. For more information, visit TypeADev.com.